The Research Report Series of the Institute for Social Research is composed of significant reports published at the completion of a research project. These reports are generally prepared by the principal research investigators and are directed to selected users of this information. Research Reports are intended as technical documents which provide rapid dissemination of new knowledge resulting from ISR research.

RESEARCH REPORT SERIES, INSTITUTE FOR SOCIAL RESEARCH

Federal Policy and the Mobility of Older Homeowners

The Effects of the One-Time Capital Gains Exclusion

Sandra Newman
Johns Hopkins University

James Reschovsky
Michigan State University

Project Manager:
Robert Marans
The University of Michigan

Survey Research Center
Institute for Social Research
The University of Michigan

1985

ISR Code No. 9020

This research was supported by the U.S. Department of Housing and Urban Development, Contract HC-5394, No. 001.

Library of Congress Cataloging in Publication Data:

Newman, Sandra J.
Federal policy and the mobility of older homeowners.

(Research report series / Institute for social research)
"ISR code no. 9020"--T.p. verso.
Bibliography: p.
1. Aged--United States--Dwellings. 2. Residential mobility--United States. 3. Capital gains tax--Law and legislation--United States. I. Reschovsky, James. II. Marans, Robert W. III. Title. IV. Series: Research report series (University of Michigan. Institute for Social Research)
HD7287.92.U54N48 1985 363.5'9 84-29745
ISBN 0-87944-302-2 (pbk.)

Published in 1985 by:

The Institute for Social Research
The University of Michigan, Ann Arbor, Michigan

6 5 4 3 2 1

Manufactured in the United States of America

Table Of Contents

Acknowledgements

We gratefully acknowledge the generous assistance of many colleagues in carrying out this research:

George Hastings (Department of Justice), Karen Sider (Office of Tax Analysis), Fritz Scheuren and Bobby Clark (Statistics on Income Division, Internal Revenue Service) answered our technical questions and provided us with information that was not readily accessible. Joe Woodworth (graduate student in Sociology, University of Michigan) provided able computer assistance in constructing the analysis file. KLB Hall (Public Policy graduate student, Johns Hopkins University) diligently researched the legislative history of Section 121 and prepared the summary that appears in Appendix A. Greg Duncan (Institute for Social Research, University of Michigan), Ray Struyk (Urban Institute), Tom Thibodeau (Southern Methodist University) and John Tuccillo (National Council of Savings and Loan Associations) helped us in the initial stages of conceptualizing the research. Richard Curtin and Laura Klem (Institute for Social Research, University of Michigan), Margery Turner (Urban Institute), the spring seminar at the Johns Hopkins Metro Center, and especially Greg Duncan helped to keep us on track both substantively and methodologically. Finally, Linda Strott (Johns Hopkins) typed the manuscript with speed and accuracy.

Executive Summary

This study represents the first systematic evaluation of the effects of the 1978 capital gains exclusion provision for older homeowners.[1] Under this version of the exclusion, formally known as Section 121 of the Internal Revenue Code, homeowners 55 and older are allowed, once in their lifetime, to exclude from gross income all of the gain up to $100,000 from the sale of a principal residence.

The legislative history of Section 121 suggests that the provision was an effort to neutralize the bias in the already existing capital gains deferral provision. The latter allows the deferral of capital gains on the sale of a home only if another home is bought and the purchase price of the new residence equals or exceeds the purchase price of the old residence. Since Congress believed that older homeowners who move are more likely to sell their homes and then either become renters or purchase a more modest dwelling, the deferral provision offered them no assistance to make such downgrading moves. Section 121 was thought to balance the incentive to upgrade by offering a tax exclusion for downgrading.

The major policy question addressed in this analysis is the extent to which Section 121 has, in fact, fostered moves by older homeowners. Two secondary effects of the provision are also examined: whether a substantial number of low-interest rate mortgages held by Section 121 claimants were rolled over as a result of induced residential moves by older homeowners, and whether there are signs of a lock-in effect on younger owners (i.e., an incentive to wait to age 55 before selling a home).

---

[1] The 1978 amendments were preceded by the original 1964 version of the law and a 1976 modification, and were followed by other amendments in 1981 which raised the excludable capital gains to $125,000.

The analysis was carried out using the Panel Study of Income Dynamics, an annual, national survey of 5,000 households begun in 1968. The sample is designed to be representative of the population as a whole, once statistical weights are applied, and subsampling does not destroy its representativeness.

The analysis file for the study was formed by pooling data for the 12 years 1970-81. This time period captures the three capital gains exclusion laws that were in effect over the decade and allows us to examine the separate effects of each of these laws.

The strategy for estimating the effects of Section 121 on mobility was to build a variable representing the effects of this policy on each household and to evaluate its contribution to a multivariate model predicting mobility. This policy variable measures the Section 121 tax savings that would accrue to each age-eligible household in the study sample if it moved. Some basic descriptive features of this tax savings variable and its components are as follows:

- --the median capital gain for households qualifying for the 1978 version of Section 121 and who sold their home after 1978 was $27,882 (in 1980 dollars). This compares with a median capital gain for those who qualified under the original version of the provision and sold their homes prior to 1977 of $8,752 (also in 1980 dollars);
- --in the 1978-80 time period, owners 55 to 64 enjoyed median tax savings that were between three to four times as great as those of owners 65 or older;
- --the level of tax savings to movers under the original 1964 provision was a small fraction of that under the 1978 amendments.

The multivariate analysis predicting mobility, which was used to estimate the size of the effects of this legislation, accounted for a wide range of indicators representing the benefits and costs of selling as well as the socioeconomic characteristics of each individual. This allowed us to control for various motivations to sell, including possibly important period effects other than the Section 121 policy intervention. Key results are as follows:

- --Section 121 has had a small, positive effect on the residential mobility of older owners, both those 55 to 64, and those 65 and older.

--For a household with mean values for all of the characteristics in the model, we estimate that the 1978 version of Section 121 was associated with an 11.4 percent increase per year in the mobility of 55 to 64 year olds over what would have taken place in the absence of the provision, and an increase of 2.8 percent over the original version for those 65 and older.

--In percentage terms, the increase for those 55 to 64 was from 3.5 to 3.9 percent, and from 3.3 to 3.6 for those 65 or older.

--In absolute terms, the number of induced moves per annum was roughly 55,000: roughly 42,000 by those 55 to 64, and 13,000 by those 65 or older.

--Assuming that only those who make downgrading moves claim the exclusion (including all moves to rental units and some (unknown) fraction of movers to less expensive owner-occupied units), our upper bound estimate on the revenue loss associated with Section 121 is $1.8 billion, while the lower bound estimate is $588 million.

--The aggregate loss and the average annual revenue loss per move is considerably higher for those 55 to 64 compared to those 65 and older.

--The tendency toward regressivity of the provision is apparent among both age groups, and the 1978 amendments may have exacerbated this tendency. However, middle-income homeowners derive the largest portion of tax savings from the provision. Measurement error may also overstate the regressivity of Section 121 because current income (the measure used here) may be higher than permanent income, and because other tax benefits available to the elderly reduce their taxable income.

--Although, at least in part, Congress based its passage of Section 121 on the assumption that the bulk of moves made by older homeowners are downgrading moves we find this not to be the case. Roughly equal fractions of owners 55 and older move to smaller and larger houses, on the one hand, and less expensive and more expensive houses, on the other. There is little systematic deviation from this tendency that is associated either with age or with the version of the provision in effect at the time of the move.

The analysis of the effects of Section 121 on younger owners was restricted to those 40 to 54 years of age. The results of this analysis include:

--the lack of any evidence for a lock-in effect on the mobility of younger owners;

--younger owners do not differ dramatically from older owners in the prevalance of upgrading versus downgrading moves. Therefore, Congress' justification for limiting Section 121 benefits to older owners -- the assumption that the primary motivation of younger owners who move is to upgrade while for older owners it is to downgrade -- is questionable.

The inducement of home sales by Section 121 also resulted in beneficial effects for the income of thrift institutions. For example, because the mortgage interest rate being paid by these post-1978 sellers on their pre-move residence was, on average, roughly 6 percentage points below the going rate, the provision was associated with the rollover of these below market rate mortgages. Further, if induced movers had the same mortgage characteristics as other movers prior to their moves and shared common post-move behavior, induced moves were likely to affect the turnover of about 25,513 mortgages per year.

Evaluating Section 121 is complicated by the fact that its fundamental goals are not clearly spelled out in the legislation and appear to conflict with one another. A policy that provides the greatest benefits to higher income homeowners who have accumulated a large amount of capital gain will not also achieve distributional goals. Similarly, the most effective strategy for increasing activity in housing markets is unlikely to be the most effective strategy for helping older homeowners with financial hardships and few housing alternatives.

To the extent that Section 121 induces some mobility among older homeowners that would not have occurred otherwise, it is likely to have three beneficial effects beyond the direct tax savings to movers. First, increased mobility by older homeowners opens up additional housing alternatives for younger households in search of larger owner-occupied homes.

Second, the rollover of below market rate mortgages benefits the mortgage industry. And third, the increased home sales activity benefits the real estate industry.

Modifying Section 121 to make it more progressive would improve equity and efficiency while also reducing the revenue loss associated with the provision. But such changes do not address the more fundamental problems with the provision, namely, confusion regarding its key objectives and its intended beneficiaries.

Chapter 1
Introduction

Since 1964, the federal government has offered a special form of financial assistance to older homeowners. Under Section 121 of the Internal Revenue Code, older taxpayers who own their homes are eligible to exclude from income some of the gain realized when the home is sold (Internal Revenue Code, 1964). Consequently, for those older homeowners who sell a personal residence on which they have realized gain, Section 121 may result in a significant tax break (Connealy, 1981).

One element in the justification given by Congress for the original version of Section 121 and its successive amendments in 1976, 1978, and 1981 was to help older homeowners fully realize the equity that they have accumulated in their homes when they found it necessary to move to smaller (and, implicitly, less expensive) dwellings (U.S. Senate, 1978a). In part, Section 121 was developed to neutralize the effects of the capital gains deferral provision (Section 1034) available to homeowners of any age (Internal Revenue Code, 1951). Congress saw elderly persons desiring to move to a more manageable and affordable residence to be in a "no win" situation. If they sold their homes and either purchased another residence costing less or became renters, they would face losing a substantial portion of the proceeds through federal capital gains taxes since the deferral provision allows the gain to be deferred only to the extent that the purchase price of the new residence exceeds the price of the old residence (U.S. Congress, Senate, 1978). The rollover provision, therefore, facilitated upgrading moves, but made downgrading moves less attractive economically. Section 121 was an effort to neutralize the bias in an existing federal tax provision that was likely to affect older homeowners adversely (Joint Committee on Taxation, 1979).

To the extent that Section 121 fosters residential moves by older owners, it may also have another effect that was not part of its original rationale: the rollover of low interest rate mortgages. One significant problem faced by the nation's thrift institutions is the large proportion of their assets that is committed to long-term, fixed rate, low interest loans. According to the President's Commission on Housing, "[A]t the end of 1980, long-term mortgages bearing interest rates below 10 percent accounted for two-thirds of all mortgages held by savings and loan associations; the proportion was even larger for mutual savings banks" (President's Commission on Housing, 1982). Many of these mortgages are held by older individuals who purchased their homes when interest rates were much lower and who have remained in these homes since that time. If the rate of home sales in this sector increased, thrift institutions would stand to benefit because these low interest mortgages could then be rolled over into higher-yield assets.[2][3] To the extent that such rollovers occur, the revenue losses of this provision as estimated by the Treasury Department might be viewed as an overstatement because they do not take these beneficial effects to the income of financial institutions into account.

This paper focuses on these intended and inadvertent consequences of Section 121. The analysis centers on the 1978 amendments which substantially liberalized the provision and increased the estimated revenue loss from under $100 million per year to more than half a billion dollars per year. With the exception of a higher dollar limit on the exclusion, this is essentially the same provision that is currently in effect.

In the next section, we describe the three different versions of Section 121 that were in effect over the decade and the broad outlines of the Congressional debate surrounding the passage of the 1978 amendments. This is followed by a review of the specific policy research questions that are the focus of this study, a description of the data set and procedures upon which the analysis is based and an overview of

---

[2] This conclusion assumes the enforcement of mandatory "due on sale" clauses.

[3] Homes free of mortgage debt, again owned primarily by older individuals, may be viewed as a subsidiary problem for thrifts since they are a potential source of mortgage revenue that is inactive. In this instance, increased sales would allow new, updated mortgages to be written.

our analysis strategy. A discussion of results is presented in the subsequent section. We conclude with an evaluation of the strengths and weaknesses of Section 121 based on the findings of this research.

Chapter 2
Mechanics and Background of Section 121[4]

Section 121 was first enacted into the Internal Revenue Code in 1964. Under this original version of the provision, homeowners who were at least 65 years old could elect, once in their lifetime, to exclude from gross income up to $20,000 in gain if they sold their principal residence. The exclusion was not complete, however: a taxpayer was allowed to exclude only part of the gain if the adjusted sales price was greater than $20,000. The excludable fraction was calculated by multiplying the gain by the ratio of $20,000 to the adjusted sales price. Thus, if the adjusted sales price was $60,000, only one-third of the gain was excludable. "Principal residence" was defined as a personal residence owned and used by the taxpayers for a period aggregating five out of the eight years preceding the sale. In 1976, in response to rising house prices, the ceiling on the exclusion was increased to $35,000 (U.S. Senate, 1976). All other elements of the provision remained the same, however.

The provision underwent a more substantial set of liberalizing revisions in 1978. First, the age of eligibility was lowered from 65 to 55 in recognition of "decreasing retirement ages" (Joint Committee on Taxation, 1979). Second, the time period during which the taxpayer owned and used the property as a principal residence was reduced to three out of five years. Third, the exclusion was increased to $100,000. And fourth, all of the gain up to $100,000 became excludable regardless of the adjusted sales price of the house. In addition to increasing the tax benefits available, this last modification also simplified the provision. In 1981, the Economic Recovery Act raised the exclusion to $125,000 (ERTA, 1981).[5]

---

[4] This section draws heavily on Connealy (1981) and Joint Committee on Taxation (1979).

The legislative history of the 1978 amendments to Section 121 provides important information on what Congress expected this provision to accomplish as well as some of its anticipated weaknesses.[6] From the perspective of this research, such information is a rich source of assumptions to be tested in evaluating the effectiveness of the provision.

The primary impression one gets from reviewing the records of the debate over the 1978 amendments is the equivocation of Congress regarding the main objectives of Section 121 and particularly who should be its beneficiaries.

Although the common view of the goal of this provision is the protection of older homeowners from heavy tax burdens when they move to less expensive houses or become renters, in fact Congress seriously considered a much more extensive role for Section 121. The House version of the amendments stated that any taxpayer, regardless of age, could elect a one-time exclusion of up to $100,000. The removal of the age limit of 65 or over was based on several factors: increasing the pool of capital flowing into savings, promoting equity between age and income groups, and preventing a "lock-in" effect among younger age groups. The thrust of this last argument is that, other things being equal, there may be an incentive for a homeowner to wait until reaching the age of eligibility for Section 121 before selling the house (U.S. Senate, 1978b).

This expansive version of the provision was actually reported to the Senate for consideration. During Senate hearings, W. Michael Blumenthal, then Secretary of the Treasury, argued strongly against this version. He based his objections on two factors: the size of the revenue loss associated with the absence of an age cap on the provision, and the view that downscaling moves primarily affect persons 55 and older, while younger owners who move already receive protection from the deferral provision because their moves are

---

[5] Adjusted sales price is defined as the selling price net of costs associated with the sale of the home (realtor fees, closing costs, etc.) as well as any repairs or improvements made to the dwelling in anticipation of or as a condition to its sale.

[6] A summary legislative history and calendar of major events are included in Appendix A.

mainly upgrading moves (U.S. Senate, 1978a). Blumenthal also argued for a $50,000 cap on the excludable gain but with no limitation on sales price.

The version of Section 121 that emerged from the Senate Committee and eventually was submitted to a joint conference committee of both Houses was a hybrid of the House expansive version and Blumenthal's more restrictive version: the Senate proposed a $50,000 cap but with no age limit. The bill ultimately reported out of the conference and later signed into law adopted the Blumenthal 55 or older age limit but with the House version's $100,000 ceiling regardless of sales price and without resort to formula. While this compromise may have been motivated largely by concerns for cost containment, it sets the focus of this evaluation on the effects of the provision on those 55 or older.

Chapter 3
Questions Addressed in this Policy Evaluation

The most fundamental question about the effects of Section 121 is whether it induced residential moves that would not have occurred otherwise. Derivative questions concern (a) the size of this effect; (b)the extent to which the effects of the 1978 amendments differed from those of the two previous laws (i.e., the 1964 and 1976 versions); (c) the distribution of benefits (that is, the characteristics of those who benefit from the provision and those who do not); and (d) the outcomes of the moves. The distribution of benefits is an important indicator of how well the provision targets those most in need. The last issue regarding outcomes relates directly to Congress' intention that this provision enable older homeowners to move to smaller and less expensive dwellings. The degree to which this intention was fulfilled can be determined by examining the size and price of post-move dwellings.

Two subsidiary questions that are relevant to an evaluation of the 1978 amendments concern younger owners (i.e., those under 55 years of age). First, to what extent were Congress' misgivings regarding the possible "lock-in" or blocked move effect for younger owners justified? Second, was the assumption that younger owners are considerably less likely to make downscaling moves correct?

The final set of questions concern the inadvertent salutary effects on thrift institutions. Measures of these effects include the degree to which the mortgage interest rate on the pre-move residence was below the going rate, and the proportion of movers who were still paying off a mortgage on their residence prior to moving.

Following the next section, in which the data set is described and several key variables are defined, we address these policy questions in roughly sequential order.

Chapter 4
Data Set, Procedures, and Key Variables

The data set used in this study is the Panel Study of Income Dynamics (PSID), a longitudinal study begun in 1968 by the Survey Research Center at the University of Michigan. The original sample of 4,802 families was composed of two subsamples. The larger portion (2,930) of the original interviews was conducted with household heads from a cross-sectional sample selected to be representative of the entire United States population. An additional 1,872 interviews were conducted with the heads of low-income households drawn from a sample identified and interviewed by the Census Bureau for the 1966 Survey of Economic Opportunity. The total response rate was 76 percent in 1968, the first year; 89 percent in the second; and at least 97 percent each year since. Families who have moved between interviews have been contacted at their new addresses. In addition, data have been collected both from the original sample families and newly formed families containing original panel members. Since 1968, the number of sample families has grown to more than 7500.

Estimates based on the total sample have been adjusted (by giving differential weights to different families) for the overrepresentation of low-income families in the original sample and for differential nonresponse rates among different subgroups in the population. Thus, the analysis presented here is based on estimates that represent (within the limits of sampling error) the status and experience of the population of interest. The sample has been designed so that subsampling does not destroy representativeness. The demographic and locational characteristics of the weighted sample are quite similar to those reported by the Census Bureau based on its 1970 Current Population Survey (CPS) (Morgan, 1972). A more recent comparison of 1977 income and demographic data from the March 1978 CPS and the PSID also showed great consistency (Morgan, 1979).

The analysis file for the study was formed by pooling data for the 12 years 1970-1981. This time period captures the three capital gains exclusion laws that were in effect over the decade, and allows us to examine the separate effects of each of these laws.[7] The unit of analysis is the household and the time period during which the probability of a home sale is estimated is the year between consecutive household interviews. The sample was restricted to households with heads 40 years of age or older (including those who reached 40 after the 1970 interview) who were owners at the beginning of each year.[8][9] The total number of observations in the resulting data set was roughly 20,000.[10]

The inclusion of households where the head was younger than 55, the minimum age required for eligibility for Section 121 benefits, was motivated by four factors. First, we were interested in examining whether the provision had any discernible effect on the mobility rates of younger households. Second, this group serves as a "control" group: those 40-54 years of age are subject to the same period effects (e.g., inflation, house price appreciation, etc.) but are ineligible for the benefits of Section 121. Third, we wanted to compare the incidence of downgrading moves by younger households to that for older households. Finally, since the version of the provision that had actually been passed by the separate House and Senate committees excluded an

---

[7] In the presentation of results, we refer to the original version of Section 121, the 1976 amendments, and the 1978 amendments, by the dates during which they were in effect: 1969-76, 1977, 1978-80, respectively.

[8] Younger owners are excluded since their mobility motivations are likely to be structurally different from owners in later life-cycle stages.

[9] Involuntary moves were excluded.

[10] Observations for each household in each year included in this analysis were treated as separate observations. Data on the household's current characteristics (t) and characteristics in the previous year (t-1) are associated with each household/year observations. This allowed us to treat each observation as a pair of years. The data set was constructed primarily from the 1981 merged family tape of the PSID. This tape contains data from all waves of the panel

age limit entirely, it is useful to examine some of the characteristics of this younger group that would have been affected by the provision had it applied to them.

Because the fundamental question examined in this analysis is the effect of Section 121 on mobility decisions, the primary dependent variable is a 1,0 measure of whether a move took place over a pair of years. Since the interviews for the PSID are conducted each spring, respondents actually report whether they have moved since the previous spring. Unfortunately, this timing does not fully overlap with the July date on which the 1978 amendments became effective. Neither does it match completely with the 1976 amendments, which took effect at the start of calendar year 1977. In constructing our key policy variable measuring the tax savings that an eligible beneficiary of Section 121 was likely to derive, we assumed that moves that took place before spring 1977 fell under the previous (and original 1964) provision. Although the mismatch between the timing of moves as reported in the PSID and the timing of the policy changes biases the results, we expect that these biases are trivial.

Our general strategy for estimating the effects of Section 121 on mobility was to build a variable representing the effects of this policy on each separate household and to evaluate its contribution to a multivariate model predicting mobility. This policy variable measures the tax savings that would accrue to each age-eligible household in the study sample if it moved.[11] For households that actually sold their

---

study through the 1981 interview year for each household that is contained in the 1981 sample. This merged family tape does not include observations for sample households who became nonrespondents in any year prior to 1981. Therefore, pre-1981 observations are not perfectly representative of the U.S. population, even when weighted. Of particular concern in this study is the exclusion of elderly households who either died or were institutionalized between 1970 and 1981. In an effort to reduce the possibly biasing effects of these drop-outs from the sample, observations on households who became non-respondents after 1975 were added from the 1975 merged family tape and weighted appropriately. This provides us with observations for the period 1970-75 for these households.

home during the period, this variable represents our estimate of the tax benefits that households derived from the Section 121 provision that was in effect at the time of the move; for households that did not sell, it represents the potential tax savings they would have enjoyed had they sold. Households not meeting the age or residency requirements for the exclusion were assigned zero values. For all other households, the magnitude of the variable is roughly a function of the capital gain on the home, the specific tax provision in effect at the time, and the household's marginal tax rate.

The median capital gain for households who qualified for Section 121 under the 1978 amendments and who sold their home during that period was $27,882 (in 1980 dollars). This compares with a median capital gain for those who qualified under the original version of the provision and sold their homes prior to 1977 of $8,752 (also in constant 1980 dollars).

Estimates of the median tax savings by age and year for all owners who moved and for those who moved into other owned homes are shown in Tables 1 and 2, respectively.[12] Both sets of estimates reveal substantial differences between age and year groups. In the 1978-80 time period, owners 55 to 64 years old enjoyed median tax savings that were between three to four times as great as those of owners 65 or older. The level of tax savings under the original rules of Section 121 was a small fraction of that under the 1978 amendments.[13]

---

[11] Appendix B presents a more complete description of the tax savings variable.

[12] Households who appear in this and subsequent tables are categorized by the age of the household head. Tax benefits under Section 121 can be claimed by either husband or wife when either one attains the age of 55. Since only 2 percent of the cases of household heads 40 to 54 years old had a spouse 55 or older, our ignoring this aspect of the provision in the analysis is unlikely to bias results.

[13] Appendix C provides several illustrative examples of the calculation of tax savings under the three versions that existed during the 1970s.

Table 1

Nominal and Real[a] Median Tax Savings
Under Section 121, By Age and Year
(movers who remained owners)

Year	55 - 64 years old		65 or older	
	Nominal (Max.)	Real (Max.)	Nominal (Max.)	Real (Max.)
1969-76	NA		$ 193 (2974)	$ 373 (4393)
			N = 66	
1977	NA		--	--
1978-80	$3081 (20708)	$3098 (22476)	$1022 (10856)	$1022 (12138)
	N = 38		N = 37	

[a]1980 dollars.

NA = Not applicable.

-- Insufficient cases.

5.4b

Table 2

Nominal and Real[a] Median Tax Savings
Under Section 121, By Age and Year
(movers who began as owners)

Year	55 - 64 years old		65 or older	
	Nominal (Max.)	Real (Max.)	Nominal (Max.)	Real (Max.)
1969 - 76	NA		$ 178 (2974)	$ 308 (4234)
			N = 101	
1977	NA		--	--
1978 - 80	$2800 (20708)	$3039 (22476)	$ 697 (10826)	$ 835 (12138)
	N = 50		N = 51	

[a]1980 dollars.

NA = not applicable.

-- Insufficient cases.

#644089

The larger tax savings enjoyed by taxpayers 55 to 64 years old relative to those 65 and over in the period after the 1978 amendments are attributable to two factors. First, the younger homeowners who moved realized slightly larger capital gains on their homes than the older homeowners. The median capital gain (in constant 1980 dollars) for movers was approximately $3000 larger for those 55 to 64 years old than for those 65 or older ($29,222 vs. $26,200). Second, and more important, is the fact that the incomes, net of proceeds from a home sale, of homeowners who moved was more than two and a half times as large for those movers in the 55 to 64 age group compared to those 65 or older (with median values of $27,000 vs. $9,512, respectively). When one considers that a sizable portion of the incomes of those 65 and over is likely to be tax free (primarily due to social security), it is consistent that the marginal tax rates of older taxpayers would be significantly lower than those of individuals 55 to 64 years old.

A final aspect of the median values of tax savings worthy of note is that these values are generally higher for owners who actually moved compared with the simulated values for owners who did not move. The estimates for nonmovers are given in Table 3. This result conforms with the expectation that it is those who have the most to gain from the tax provision who are also those most likely to move.[14]

---

[14] The extent to which this may reflect nonmovers' underestimation of their house value is not known.

Table 3

Simulated Nominal and Real[a] Median Tax Savings
Under Section 121, By Age and Year
(nonmovers who remained owners)

Year	55 - 64 years old		65 or older	
	Nominal (Max.)	Real (Max.)	Nominal (Max.)	Real (Max.)
1969 - 76	NA		$ 175 (3900)	$ 297 (6603)
			N = 2770	
1977	NA		$ 563 (9431)	$ 735 (12302)
			N = 434	
1978 - 80	$2320 (31518)	$2518 (37725)	$ 821 (24600)	$ 900 (24600)
	N = 1403		N = 1498	

[a]1980 dollars.

NA = Not applicable.

5.4b

Chapter 5
Results

Effects on Mobility

Table 4 shows the aggregate mobility rates for the different age and year groups that have policy relevance in this evaluation. The proportion of older homeowners who moved appears to have remained essentially stable over the decade and, therefore, over the period encompassing the three different versions of Section 121. Of course, these aggregates are not terribly revealing and may hide potentially dramatic differences in the influences on the mobility streams of each of these age and/or year groups, including, perhaps, the effects of Section 121.

Our approach to estimating the effects of Section 121 was to include the policy variable, tax savings, in a predictive model of residential mobility. Although our main concern is with the size, direction, and significance of this policy variable, the accuracy of these estimates is directly affected by the appropriateness of the general mobility model in which the policy variable is embedded. Stated somewhat differently, since we are attempting to isolate the effects of Section 121 over and above other potentially important influences on residential mobility, these other influences must be controlled for properly.

Our model estimates the likelihood that a given household will move during a given year. Coefficient estimates, then, relate the explanatory variables to the probability of moving. The dependent variable is dichotomous: movers are assigned a value of 1 and others are assigned 0's. Ordinary least squares regression is inappropriate when the dependent variable is of this form. Therefore, we estimated the model using logit analysis, a maximum likelihood estimation technique. In the logit model, the probability that a household will move is estimated as the cumulative density function of the standard logistic function.[15]

---

[15] The major problems associated with ordinary least squares

Table 4

Mobility Rates By Age Group and Year
(owners only)

Age	1969-76	1977	1978-80
40 - 54 years old	.06	.06	.04
(N)	(6409)	(846)	(2577)
55 - 64 years old	.04	.05	.04
(N)	(3177)	(459)	(1474)
65 or older	.03	.04	.04
(N)	(2912)	(455)	(1578)

#618076

We adopted a benefit/cost framework to model the mobility decision.[16] The benefits of moving derive from the fact that the characteristics of the current home and neighborhood may be at variance with desired housing characteristics (i.e., those the household would select if it were to move). The variance between current and desired levels of housing consumption results because the household's demand for housing is likely to change over time in response to changes in family size and composition, income, aspirations, and the like. Households fail to readily make adjustments in their current housing since there are significant costs to moving: the costs of moving belongings, transactions costs, search costs and the costs associated with leaving familiar surroundings and friends. Moves, then, should occur when the benefits of moving (evaluated over the household's decision horizon) outweigh the costs. Since we cannot directly measure these benefits or costs, the variables in the model are indicators of those benefits and costs (i.e., variables that we hypothesize to be related to the benefits or costs of moving).

The mobility model was estimated several times using alternative indicators of benefit and cost variables. Consistently insignificant predictors were excluded from the final specification. The coefficient on the policy variable, tax savings, proved to be insensitive to the specification used.

---

regression where the dependent variable is binary are heteroscedasticity and the possibility that predicted values of Y, the dependent variable, will fall outside the 0,1 range. Such values would be inconsistent with the definitions of Y. The consequence of these difficulties is that standard significance tests do not hold.

[16] This approach is a simplified and more modest version of the one pursued by Reschovsky (1982).

[17] The testing and searching process was done on a random half sample of the data set. Final estimates were run on the full sample rather than the other half sample, however, in order to maximize sample sizes on key variables. This approach yields the best possible estimates of the effects of Section 121 on

Our final mobility model contained 21 predictors.[17] Indicators of benefits to be derived from moving (or, more generally, factors that may predispose a household to move) included characteristics of the pre-move residence (over- or under-consumption of space) and demographic and socioeconomic characteristics of the household. The latter encompassed measures of change in family composition, marital status, and retirement status, and the age, sex, race and income of the head of household. Two measures represented the costs to moving: length of residence, which connotes the extent of connectedness to the home and neighborhood, and the price discount associated with owning a home carrying a mortgage interest rate below the going rate.[18] In order to control for potentially important period effects on mobility other than Section 121, three measures of macroeconomic conditions characterizing the year prior to the move were included: the unemployment rate, inflation rate, and real interest rate. The full list of variables and their coding schemes is included in Appendix B.

Because of our interest in calculating whether the different versions of Section 121 were differentially effective and also whether different age groups had distinct responses to the provision, we estimated the model three times: once on all age groups pooled together, and then separately on those 55 to 64 years old and those 65 or older.

The resulting coefficients on the policy variable are given in Table 5. These estimates indicate that the Section 121 capital gains exclusion has had a small, positive effect on the residential mobility of older owners. The separate age group estimates show that this conclusion applies to both age groups.[19]

---

mobility but it violates the assumptions on which the significance tests are based. T tests, therefore, should be interpreted cautiously.

[18] The construction of the price discount variable is discussed in Appendix B.

[19] Although these estimates are not significant at conventional levels, the significance tests are very sensitive to sample sizes. More importantly, and as noted earlier, the

Table 5

Logit Coefficients, T Statistics, and
Significance of Policy Variable, Tax Savings,
For All Age Groups, 55-64 Year Olds, and 65 or Older

Age Group	B	T Statistic	Significance Level
All pooled	.0500	2.98	.01
55 - 64 years old	.0335	1.42	~.15
65 or older	.0623	1.44	~.15

5.6

Estimates of the size of these effects -- the proportion of moves induced by Section 121 that would not have occurred in its absence -- were calculated for an "average" individual from each of the separate age group samples (i.e., having average values on all indicators, including tax savings, as estimated for the study samples. These mean values for the three samples are listed in Appendix D.)

It is important to emphasize that the use of mean values to calculate the size of Section 121 effects and its cost implications produces hypothetical estimates only. While assigning mean values is defensible on practical grounds, the implication that all individuals conform to the average may be problematic. If Section 121 effects differ substantially depending on particular individual attributes (e.g., for high versus low education individuals), the assumption that everyone is at the mean is incorrect. In the absence of further detailed analysis of such sub-group effects, the assignment of mean values is no more or less arbitrary than any other approach, but its possible limitations must be recognized.

The results of these calculations are summarized in Table 6. For heads of households 55 to 64 years old who were homeowners, the 1978 version of Section 121 was associated with an 11.4 percent increase in mobility over what would have taken place if the provision did not exist. For those 65 and older, the comparable estimate is 9 percent. However, since this older group was already able to claim the tax forgiveness of a previous version of Section 121, this rate overestimates the effects of the 1978 amendments. A more appropriate estimated increase in mobility rates is one based on the previous provision rather than no provision at all. This more accurate estimate for older owners is 2.8 percent.[20]

---

significance tests must be examined cautiously because of our approach to this analysis.

[20] This estimate is based on the difference between the original version of Section 121 and the 1978 amendments. The 1976 amendment was not used due to small sample sizes for the single year in which this version was in effect.

Table 6

Percentage Increase in Mobility
Induced by Section 121,
by Age and Version of Provision[a]

Provision	Age Group: 55 - 64 years old	Age Group: 65 or older	
No Provision			
Original Provision (i.e., $20,000 exclusion)		.2%	
1978 Provision (i.e., $100,000 exclusion)	.4%	.1%	.3%

Thus, % increase in mobility:

	55 - 64 years old	65 or older
-- from no provision	11.4%	9.0%
-- from original provision	NA	2.8%

[a]Based on individual at mean values for all independent variables in logit model and unrounded mobility rates listed in Table 1. (See Appendix D for listing of all variables and means.)

NA = not applicable.

5.4a

Another note of caution is in order at this point. Since standard errors of our estimated logit coefficient on the tax savings variable are fairly large in relation to the size of the coefficient, the actual impact of Section 121 on mobility may vary significantly from those reported here.

While the percentage increases appear to be sizable, particularly in the case of owners 55 to 64 years old, it is important to remember that they are based on small aggregate mobility rates. Therefore, the probability of an average homeowner 55 to 64 years old moving during that year increased from 3.5 percent to 3.9 percent as a result of the 1978 amended version of Section 121. For owners 65 or older, the increase associated with applying the 1978 version of Section 121 as opposed to its original version was from 3.5 percent to 3.6 percent. Translating these estimated proportions of moves induced by Section 121 into aggregates produced roughly 55,000 additional moves by households headed by someone 55 and older: roughly 42,000 by those 55 to 64 years old, and about 13,000 by those 65 and older.[21,22]

Estimates of the total revenue loss associated with this provision vary substantially depending upon the assumptions that are made about who actually claims the exclusion. Since the benefit of this provision is an exclusion from federal taxes, the Internal Revenue Service and Office of Tax Analysis in the Treasury Department believe that only a fraction of those who have benefited from the provision in fact have also

---

[21] Based on applying the predicted mobility rates from the logits for each age group to the total number of owners in the population in each age group (U.S. Department of Commerce, 1982).

[22] While this analysis indicates that Section 121 has had only a modest effect on the mobility of older homeowners, it does not indicate whether the provision has affected the type of moves that are taking place. In a subsequent analysis, we used multinominal logit to simultaneously test the influence of Section 121 on the decision to move and the decision to upgrade versus downgrade. The results do not support the hypothesis that Section 121 encourages downgrading moves. For a more complete review of this analysis, see Newman and Reschovsky, 1984.

actually filed IRS Form 2119 (U.S. Department of the Treasury, 1984a; 1984b). There are also no reliable data on how filers differ from non-filers or the proportion of those who file. Therefore, IRS claims data may underestimate the effects of Section 121. Our estimates, on the other hand, are not restricted to those who file Form 2119. But since we do not know who has actually derived Section 121 benefits, our estimates are only as reasonable as the assumptions on which they are based.

Because the provision makes the most economic sense for owners who downgrade (i.e., move to units of lesser value), an upper bound estimate can be derived by assuming that all owners who downgrade when they move claim the exclusion. The definition of downgrading remains the same as in our earlier analysis, and includes all moves to rental units plus moves to owned units with market values that are lower than the previously owned primary residence.

Setting the parameters for a lower bound estimate is more arbitrary. Our strategy was to maintain the assumption that all movers to rental units used Section 121 but to assume that only a fraction of those moving to other owner-occupied units did so. In our lowest estimate, we assumed that only 20 percent of all such moves benefited from Section 121, but this rate is arbitrary and others may be equally or more reasonable.

The resulting range of cost estimates is shown in Table 7.[23] The estimated total annual revenue loss, reported in the third data column is, in most cases, substantially higher than the various estimates reported by the Senate Budget and Finance Committees or the Joint Committee on Taxation (see Appendix A, Table A-1). Only when the proportion of claims by movers to other owned homes is reduced to 20 percent is the total loss figure in the same range as these Congressional estimates. (An average of the Office of Management and Budget estimates for the same time period is roughly $500 million per year.)

---

[23] An estimate of the benefits of Section 121, such as the beneficial effects on thrift institutions, is not taken into account in either our estimates or those of the Treasury Department.

Table 7

Estimated Annual Revenue Loss Associated With Section 121 (1978 Amendments)[a]

Assumptions	Total Loss			Loss Per Move		
	55-64 Year Olds	65 or Older	All	55-64 Year Olds	65 or Older	All
I. S.121 claimed by all owners 55+ who downgraded (i.e., moved to either rental units or owned homes of lower market value)	$1.1 bil.	$726 mil.	$1.8 bil.	$5843	$2898	$4166
(Number of Claimants)				(189393)	(250531)	(439924)
II. S.121 claimed by all owners 55+ who moved to rental units and by 70% of owners who downgraded	$817 mil.	$549 mil.	$1.4 bil.	$5364	$2704	$3845
(Number of Claimants)				(152348)	(202880)	(355228)
III. S.121 claimed by all owners 55+ who moved to rental units and by 50% of owners who downgraded	$624 mil.	$430 mil.	$1.1 bil.	$4890	$2515	$3530
(Number of Claimants)				(127651)	(171113)	(298764)
IV. S.121 claimed by all owners 55+ who moved to rental units and by 20% of owners who downgraded	$335 mil.	$253 mil.	$588 mil.	$3705	$2049	$2745
(Number of Claimants)				(90608)	(123461)	(214069)

[a]Aggregate number of movers between 1981 and 1982 taken from U.S. Department of Commerce (1982). Estimates on downgraders and average tax savings per move per year between 1978 and 1980 derived from special tabulations from the PSID study file. The latter estimates were derived separately by age (55-64 and 65 or older) and post-move tenure (rent versus own), but the separate tenure estimates were reaggregated for the final presentation.

Another noteworthy aspect of these figures is the higher average annual revenue loss per move for those 55 to 64 years old versus those 65 or older. As noted previously, the older group is entitled to other tax benefits that reduce their marginal tax rates and thereby reduce the amount of tax savings to be gained from this tax provision.

As expected, the highest average loss per move ($4166) occurs under the assumption of Section 121 benefit claims by all downgraders, while the lowest ($2745) arises when it is assumed that only 20 percent of downgrading owners claim benefits. Even the upper bound estimate, however, is about $2500 smaller than the average cost per move that is produced by the Office of Tax Analysis numbers: 85,000 movers and an annual loss of about $570 million (or $6729 per move).[24] This discrepancy again highlights the importance of the assumptions regarding who claims the exclusion and who files Form 2119.

Distribution of Benefits

Our main interest in examining the distribution of benefits from Section 121 is the extent to which the amount of tax savings derived from the provision is associated with the taxpayer's income. Because the provision was modified during the decade, it is also of interest to see whether the distribution of benefits differed under alternative versions of the provision or systematically by age of taxpayer. Since the tax savings variable has values for all cases of age-eligible movers regardless of whether they file IRS Form 2119 to declare their use of the capital gains exclusion, it fills an important void in IRS data which has information on only a fraction of home sales and no age-specific information on this form of exclusion income (Congressional Budget Office, 1981).

The relationship between tax savings and income under the 1978 version of Section 121 is shown in Table 8. Although the cell frequencies are small, there is a clear tendency for tax savings to increase as income rises.

Table 9 shows the distribution of tax benefits separately for those 65 and older, who were the ongoing beneficiaries of the one-time exclusion, and those 55 to 64 years old, who became eligible for the exclusion under the 1978 amendments. Though we are again troubled by small case counts, the

---

[24] 1982 estimates (U.S. Department of the Treasury, 1984b).

Table 8

Real[a] Tax Savings Under Section 121,
By Income
(movers 55 or older in 1978-80 only)

Tax Savings	Income[b]			
	< $10,000	$10,000-19,999	$20,000-39,999	$40,000 or more
$0	49.3%	26.3%	15.4%	16.4%
< $3500	48.4	44.9	29.5	13.8
$3500 or more	2.3	28.7	55.1	69.8
	100.0%	100.0%	100.0%	100.0%
(N)	(34)	(21)	(28)	(14)

tau-b=.445

tau-c=.465

[a]1980 dollars.

[b]Net of proceeds from home sale.

#618076

Table 9

Real[a] Tax Savings Under Section 121,
By Age and Income
(movers in 1978 - 80 only)

Tax Savings	Income[b]			
55 - 64 years old:	< $10,000	$10,000-19,999	$20,000-39,999	$40,000 or more
$0	23.3%	31.7%	12.7%	12.5%
< $3500	76.7	62.5	33.0	17.2
$3500 or more	...	5.8	54.4	70.3
	100.0%	100.0%	100.0%	100.0%
(N)	(9)	(10)	(18)	(11)
				tau-b=.412 tau-c=.413
65 or older:				
$0	55.2%	22.6%	19.7%	--
< $3500	42.0	32.9	23.9	--
$3500 or more	2.8	44.5	56.3	--
	100.0%	100.0%	100.0%	--
(N)	(25)	(11)	(10)	--
				tau-b=.435 tau-c=.426

[a]1980 dollars.

[b]Net of proceeds from home sale.

-- Insufficient cases.

... Zero cases.

#618076

tendency toward regressivity is apparent among both age groups.

The 1978 amendments may have made the provision somewhat more regressive, however. As shown in Table 10, which displays the distribution of benefits for those 65 and older under the original version of Section 121 and its 1978 amended version, the magnitude of inflation-adjusted tax benefits enjoyed by higher income individuals increased under the later provision.[25]

How one interprets these findings depends in part on how one views the measure of income. Although the tax benefits associated with the provision tend to rise as income rises, it is also the case that the income class deriving the largest portion of tax savings defines what is usually considered middle-income rather than high income (i.e., up to $40,000 income). This interpretation is consistent with the Congressional Budget Office conclusions that many older people with expensive homes do not have very high incomes and that 85 percent of those 55 and older selling homes have incomes of $30,000 or less (Congressional Budget Office, 1981). Therefore, the provision may in fact be targeting middle income households and the characterization of the provision as truly regressive may not be appropriate. Measurement error in our income variable may also overstate the regressivity of the provision. If our real interest is in how the benefits of this provision are distributed across taxpayers at different levels of financial status, then current income may not be the most appropriate indicator of economic well-being. This is particularly the case for taxpayers 65 and older for two main reasons. First, those 65 and older have lower consumption needs than younger individuals and are more likely to be deriving a larger portion of their income from non-taxed, in-kind sources. A primary source is imputed rental income from home equity (roughly 85 percent of older owners own their homes free and clear of mortgage debt). This suggests that permanent income might be a more appropriate measure than annual money income which was used in this analysis. Permanent income would produce values that are lower than annual income. Second, those 65 and older enjoy smaller tax

---

[25] Insufficient cases precluded an examination of the 1976 amendments.

Table 10

Real[a] Tax Savings Under Alternative
Tax Provisions for Sellers 65 or Older,
By Income
(movers)

Tax Savings	Income[b]			
1969 - 76	< $10,000	$10,000-19,999	$20,000-39,999	$40,000 or more
$0	25.8%	39.9%	31.8%	--
< $3500	74.2	60.1	68.3	--
$3500 or more	...	...	...	--
	100.0%	100.0%	100.0%	--
(N)	(30)	(37)	(11)	--
				tau-b=.046 tau-c=.038
1978 - 80				
$0	55.2%	22.6%	19.7%	--
< $3500	42.0	32.9	23.9	--
$3500 or more	2.8	44.5	56.3	--
	100.0%	100.0%	100.0%	--
(N)	(25)	(11)	(10)	--
				tau-b=.435 tau-c=.426

[a] 1980 dollars.

[b] Net of proceeds from home sale.

[c] $20,000 exclusion (see text for details).

[d] $100,000 exclusion (see text for details).

-- Insufficient cases.

... Zero cases.

#618076

savings from Section 121 largely because their tax liabilities are much lower. In addition to having lower incomes, social security payments are not taxed and extra exemptions are available.

Mobility Outcomes: Characteristics of Post-Move Dwellings

It will be recalled that in the Congressional debate over the 1978 amendments, a fundamental component in the argument to restrict Section 121 benefits to older homeowners was the belief that residential moves to less expensive and smaller dwellings comprised the main kinds of moves undertaken by older taxpayers. It was for this reason that Section 1034, the capital gains deferral that facilitates upgrading moves, was viewed as not meeting the needs of older movers.

Whether the proponents of this view were correct can be derived from a comparison of the price and size of post-move dwellings relative to pre-move dwellings. For the size comparisons, we looked at all owners who moved whether they remained owners or became renters. For the price comparisons, we included two groups in our definition of those who downgrade: owners who purchased other homes with lower house values than the home sold, and all owners who became renters.[26]

Both comparisons suggest that the moves of older owners are not particularly well-characterized as downgrading moves. In terms of proportions, roughly an equal fraction of owners 55 and older move to smaller and larger houses, on the one hand, and less expensive and more expensive houses, on the other. Owners 65 and over are somewhat more likely to conform to the downgrading scenario but this tendency is only slight. Neither is there evidence for any systematic variation associated with the version of Section 121 in effect at the time of the move.

The finding of substantial upgrading in older ages is surprising. It may partially be explained by measurement error since respondents who are removed from housing market activities may underestimate the value of their property. Therefore, respondents may underestimate the value of their

---

[26] It should be noted that more than three-fourths of all owners 55 or older purchase other owned homes when they move.

homes prior to their move. However, Census data indicate that the homes owned by elderly residents tend to have relatively low market values since they are more likely to be old structures and located in undesirable neighborhoods.

The proportion of moves that involve an increase in housing investment is important in gauging the significance of Section 121 to older homeowners. Households who move into owner-occupied houses that have higher market values than those they left need not take advantage of the tax forgiveness provision since they are able to roll over their accumulated capital gain into the new home. Homeowners who move to less expensive houses, however, may have the incentive to use the provision. If the exemption is not elected, they would have to pay taxes on the gain up to the amount of difference between the new house price and the adjusted sales price of the prior residence. Yet, for those who are only modestly downgrading, who can anticipate additional appreciation on their new home, and who can anticipate moving from their new residence, it may be reasonable to pay taxes on a portion of the capital gain accumulated thus far and not elect to use the one-time exclusion at that time. Unfortunately, we cannot determine, a priori, which households in our sample actually elected Section 121.

These results are summarized in the lower two panels of Tables 11 to 14.[27] Table 11 indicates that the inflation-adjusted median value of post-move residences is generally equal to or greater than that of the principal residence that was sold. Table 12 conveys this same message in a somewhat different way by showing the incidence of moves to less expensive dwellings.

These figures are consistent with those that describe the size of houses sold and purchased by older owners. First, Table 13 shows the average change in the number of rooms between the pre- and post-move residences. While the mean change is negative (that is, in the direction of fewer rooms), it is also very small, generally approaching a decrease in size of only one room. This order of magnitude is not what is commonly considered a downsizing move. Second, as shown in

---

[27] The upper panel reports the estimates for younger households and will be discussed in a later section of this report.

Table 11

Median Real[a] House Value Pre- and Post-Move,
By Age and Year
(movers who remained owners)

Age	1969-76 Pre-Move Residence	1969-76 Post-Move Residence	1977 Pre-Move Residence	1977 Post-Move Residence	1978-80 Pre-Move Residence	1978-80 Post-Move Residence
40 - 54 years old	$40,845	$55,142	$65,225	$84,792	$50,870	$75,977
[s][b]	[28283]	[36357]	[27632]	[46639]	[59158]	[71419]
	(N = 252)		(N = 39)		(N = 65)	
55 - 64 years old	$36,761	$47,843	--	--	$53,862	$75,000
[s][b]	[29119]	[32956]			[35470]	[37832]
	(N = 90)				(N = 38)	
65 or older	$31,120	$32,249	--	--	$41,892	$47,877
[s][b]	[30800]	[27807]			[41261]	[55564]
	(N = 66)				(N = 37)	

[a]1980 dollars.

[b][s] represents the standard deviation.

-- Insufficient cases.

5.4b

Table 12

Proportion of Moves to
Less Expensive Dwellings,
By Age and Year
(movers who downgraded)[a]

Age	Year 1969-76	Year 1977	Year 1978-80
40 - 54 years old	.49	.38	.52
(N)	(358)	(48)	(107)
55 - 64 years old	.44	.70	.46
(N)	(122)	(16)	(50)
65 or older	.63	.62	.52
(N)	(101)	(16)	(51)

[a]See text for definitions.

5.12

Table 13

Mean Change in Number of Rooms
Between Pre- and Post-Move Year,
By Age and Year
(movers who began as owners)

Age	Year 1969-76	Year 1977	Year 1978-80
40 - 54 years old	- .21	- .81	-1.04
(N)	(255)	(39)	(83)
55 - 64 years old	- .29	-1.07	- .29
(N)	(97)	(15)	(46)
65 or older	- .84	- .81	- .97
(N)	(80)	(16)	(45)

4.23
4.25

Table 14

Proportion of Moves to Smaller Dwellings,[a]

By Age and Year

(movers who began as owners)

Age	Year 1969-76	Year 1977	Year 1978-80
40 - 54 years old	37%	47%	50%
(N)	(225)	(39)	(83)
55 - 64 years old	32%	40%	43%
(N)	(97)	(15)	(46)
65 or older	47%	42%	58%
(N)	(80)	(16)	(45)

[a]Measured by number of rooms in the dwelling. Dwellings of equal size were included with larger dwellings.

#622799;4.25

Table 14, the incidence of moves to smaller dwellings is also just about equal to that for moves into larger houses. As with house prices, the tendency for downsizing is somewhat more likely at older ages but even in these instances, this tendency is very modest.[28] Other tabulations suggest that the clearest evidence of downgrading moves may be concentrated among owners who became renters. (These data are not presented due to very small cell sizes.) Comparing number of rooms before and after a move shows that the large majority of moves do, in fact, involve downsizing. But the average decrease is still only about one room, again not conforming to the general view of what constitutes major downsizing.

Section 121 and Younger Households

Because we set the minimum age for our study sample at 40 years old, we were only able to test the Congressional assumptions regarding Section 121 and younger taxpayers on this subgroup of younger individuals. Our findings, therefore, refer only to owners between the ages of 40 and 54.[29]

Effects on Mobility

We could find no evidence to support Congress' misgiving about a possible lock-in effect on the mobility of younger owners that related to the age-eligibility restriction of Section 121. We searched for such evidence by reestimating the logit regression model predicting the probability of a residential move on the subsample of 40 to 54 year olds. The predictors remained essentially the same as in the models for the older age groups but with one exception. The tax savings variable, which had a zero value for all of these younger sample members, was dropped. In its place, two alternative

---

[28] Tables E-1 and E-2 indicate the even more modest extent of downsizing among the large majority of older owners who buy other homes after they move.

[29] These findings could be generalized to younger owners only if one were convinced that the housing market behavior of owners younger than 40 were the same as that of owners 40 or older. As noted earlier, the evidence suggests that there are substantial differences between these groups.

sets of indicators of Section 121 effects were substituted: dummy variables for the groupings of years that represented the different versions of the tax provision, and an interaction term between accumulated capital gains to date and number of years remaining until age 55 (the first opportunity to claim Section 121 benefits). This latter variable appears to capture directly why a lock-in effect might result: it is those owners who have most to gain within the shortest period of time who should also be most influenced by the provision.

The results of these analyses indicate that Section 121 does not have significant effects for individuals who do not yet qualify for its benefits. The coefficient on the interaction term was insignificant, indicating that no combination of likely tax savings and years until these could be realized made a difference in the mobility decisions of younger owners. Further, if one or more versions of Section 121 had blocked the moves of younger owners, the year dummies should have had significant negative coefficients indicating declines in mobility rates. These effects were not found.[30] A very different effect which we did not test relates to an evaluation of both Section 121 and Section 1034 (the deferral provision for homeowners regardless of age): younger homeowners who have large capital gains and who move may purchase more expensive homes than they otherwise would have in order to avoid the capital gains tax.

Characteristics of Residential Moves

In addition to the concern expressed in Congress regarding the potential lock-in effects of Section 121 on younger households, Congress' decision to restrict Section 121 benefits to older households was partly based on the

---

[30] The lack of support for the assumption of blocked moves in the year dummies regression was especially strong since the coefficient on the dummy variable for the year 1977 was actually positive and significant. We have no explanation for this result. It seems unlikely to be related either to Section 121, because of the results from the second regression, or to macroeconomic conditions, since these were taken into account. It may be some noneconomic factor(s) related to 1977 that is unique to these data but not applicable to the underlying population.

assumption that it is older homeowners who make downgrading moves. The logical extension of this argument, and one that was actually presented by Treasury Secretary Blumenthal, is that younger owners mainly undertake upgrading moves and therefore benefit from the capital gains rollover provision (Section 1034) (U.S. Senate, 1978b). In a previous section, we examined whether the characterization of older owners' moves was accurate and concluded that the incidence of downgrading moves was just about equal to the incidence of upgrading moves. Our parallel analysis on owners younger than 55 leads to roughly the same conclusion, as shown in the top panels of Tables 11 through 14. These figures indicate that: (a) the median inflation-adjusted value of homes purchased by younger owners who sell a primary residence is substantially higher than that of the pre-move residence; (b) the incidence of moves to higher priced and lower priced dwellings is roughly equal; (c) on average, younger owners move to dwellings that are somewhat smaller than the ones they have sold; but (d) overall, the incidence of moves to smaller dwellings is about the same as that to larger ones.

More important than these estimates for younger owners, per se, is what they imply about the targeting of Section 121. Since there are few discernible differences in the prevalence of upgrading versus downgrading moves by younger versus older owners, Congress' justification for limiting Section 121 benefits to older owners is questionable. There may be other persuasive arguments for targeting the age eligibility of the provision on those 55 and older, but distinctions based on the characteristics of moves do not fall into this category.

Financial Effects of Section 121

The final set of effects to be evaluated concern the extent to which the capital gains exclusion for older homeowners has had salutary effects on the mortgage market. These effects can be examined in several ways.

First, for owners who were still holding mortgages on the homes that they sold under each version of Section 121, we can compare the interest rate on the property sold with the going rate in the market to determine whether the two were substantially different from each other. The results of these calculations are shown in Table 15 by age and policy-relevant year. In the earlier part of the decade, mortgage interest rates on homes sold averaged only one or two points below the

Table 15

Average Mortgage Interest Rate on
Pre-Move Residence vs. Going Rate,
By Age and Year
(movers who began as owners)

Age Group	Going Rate:	1969-76	1977	1978-80
		.086	.097	.139
55 - 64 years old		.07	--	.08
(N)		(45)		(28)
[% w/mortgage]		[45%]		[61%]
65 or older		.07	--	.08
(N)		(22)		(14)
[% w/mortgage]		[25%]		[24%]
Persons 40 - 54 years old		.07	.08	.09
(N)		(177)	(35)	(62)
[% w/mortgage]		[78%]	[85%]	[74%]

-- Insufficient cases.

5.16

going rate. The sharp increases in interest rates in the economy in the 1978-80 period, however, increased the differential to six percentage points.

The table also provides information on another issue that is salient for evaluating this particular set of effects, namely, that a sizable proportion of older owners who sold their principal residences were still holding mortgages on these properties. This means that the pool of mortgages to be rolled over was substantial. While only about one-fourth of sellers 65 and older held mortgages, this proportion rises to 61 percent for those 55 to 64. In addition, in the 1978-80 period, all owners 55 and older who held a mortage on the property they sold had an average of about $15,600 in principal remaining to be paid.

A final feature of Table 15 concerns younger owners. Once again, their mortgage characteristics do not differ dramatically from those of owners in the 55 to 64 year age range though they are more likely to hold a mortgage on their home.

The focus of Table 15 is the pre-move residence and the beneficial effects derived from the rollover of mortgages once these homes were sold. Beneficial effects are also associated with the mortgage market activity centered on the post-move residence for those older owners who purchase other homes. As shown in Table 16, the large majority of sellers in every age and year group bought other homes rather than rented, thereby generating a substantial amount of mortgage activity by taking out mortgage loans for the post-move residence. If the mortgages on all of these newly purchased homes were written at the going rate, the estimates given in Table 17 would result. Not surprisingly, Table 17 indicates that the proportion of movers who held mortgage loans on the homes they sold was lower than the proportion taking out a loan for the residence that was purchased.

Given our estimates of the effects of Section 121 on mobility, we predict that an additional 55,464 moves were induced annually by the 1978 amendments. If we assume that induced movers had the same mortgage characteristics as other movers prior to their moves and shared common post-move behavior, induced moves were likely to affect the turnover of

Table 16

Post-Move Tenure,
By Year and Age Group
(movers who were owners only)

	Post Move Tenure											
	1969-76				1977				1978-80			
Age	Own	Rent	Neither	Total	Own	Rent	Neither	Total	Own	Rent	Neither	Total
40 - 54 years of age	72.1	25.9	2.0	100.0 (358)	79.5	15.9	4.6	100.0 (48)	64.0	29.8	6.2	100.0 (107)
55 - 64 years of age	75.0	19.5	5.5	100.0 (122)	50.3	45.6	4.1	100.0 (16)	80.1	16.0	3.8	100.0 (50)
65 or older	63.9	27.8	8.3	100.0 (101)	52.5	36.6	10.9	100.0 (16)	73.5	19.0	7.5	100.0 (51)

#618701

Table 17

Pre- and Post-Move Average Mortgage Interest Rates,
By Age and Year
(movers who remained owners)

Age	1969-76 Pre-Move Residence	1969-76 Post-Move Residence	1977 Pre-Move Residence	1977 Post-Move Residence	1978-80 Pre-Move Residence	1978-80 Post-Move Residence
40 - 54 years old	.07	.09	.08	.10	.08	.13
(N)	(128)	(217)	(30)	(36)	(37)	(52)
[% w/mortgage]	[77%]	[85%]	[85%]	[93%]	[68%]	[79%]
55 - 64 years old	.06	.09	--	--	.08	.14
(N)	(35)	(55)	--	--	(37)	(25)
[% w/mortgage]	[47%]	[53%]			[66%]	[69%]
65 or older	.07	.09	--	--	--	--
(N)	(17)	(24)	--	--	--	--
[% w/mortgage]	[28%]	[33%]	--	--		

-- Insufficient cases.

#618076

about 25,513 mortgages per year.[31]

One last set of financial data are the characteristics of the mortgages held by the pool of homeowners who remain eligible for Section 121 benefits because they have not moved from their principal residence since July 1978. While many of these owners may never sell and therefore never receive the tax forgiveness of this provision, for those who do sell, it is useful to assess whether their current mortgage loans are below the going rate and by how much. This information is given in Table 18 which shows for the single year 1980, the average mortgage interest rate on loans held by owners 55 and over who had not sold their principal residence since the effective date of the 1978 version of Section 121. The differential is a dramatic 10 percentage points. Substituting the average mortgage interest on owner-occupied single family homes that is currently in effect (about 12 percent) reduces this differential to six percentage points.

[31] The magnitude of this effect is not likely to be very large, however, since older homeowners have generally paid off a substantial portion, if not all, of their mortgage principal.

Table 18

1980 Average Mortgage Interest Rates of Owners Who Have Not Moved Since 1978, By Age

	Average Mortgage Interest Rate	Going Rate = 16.6%
All 55 or older	.06	
(N)	(964)	
55 - 59 years old	.07	
(N)	(234)	
60 - 64 years old	.06	
(N)	(220)	
65 - 69 years old	.06	
(N)	(194)	
70 - 74 years old	.06	
(N)	(137)	
75 or older	.06	
(N)	(179)	

#618076

Chapter 6
Summary and Conclusions

Evaluating the capital gains exclusion is complicated by the fact that its fundamental goals are not clearly spelled out in the legislation and appear to conflict with one another. Is Section 121 primarily a policy to help older homeowners with the greatest needs? Or was it most fundamentally an attempt to neutralize the bias in the tax code that may have discouraged downgrading moves? Or is it a policy to generate greater housing market activity generally? While each of these goals may be worth pursuing, a policy that provides the greatest benefits to higher-income homeowners who have accumulated a large amount of capital gain will not also achieve distributional goals. Similarly, the most effective strategy for increasing fluidity in housing markets is unlikely to be the most effective strategy for assisting older homeowners with financial hardships and few housing alternatives.

In view of these problems with the identification and consistency of policy goals, we have chosen to review what Section 121 appears to have achieved, what its major weaknesses seem to be, and whether some modification to the provision makes sense.

In passing the capital gains exclusion provision, one of the stated purposes of Congress was to offer assistance to long-term older homeowners who wished to move to more manageable and affordable housing units. This evaluation suggests that the provision has facilitated residential moves that might not have occurred in its absence. The 1978 amendments to Section 121 have generated approximately 55,000 additional moves per year by households whose heads are 55 years of age or older; this represents an increase of roughly six percent in the aggregate number of moves.

While this policy does not involve federal budget outlays, it does have its costs. These take the form of revenues not collected because the provision allows the exclusion of accumulated capital gains from federal income taxes. Estimates of the total revenue loss as a result of

Section 121 depend heavily on the assumptions concerning which movers elect to use the provision. Overall, the range is likely to have been between $588 million and somewhat more than $1 billion per year during the early 1980s. Without additional research to determine who actually claims Section 121, neither IRS data nor any other existing data bases can provide more than rough approximations based on alternative sets of assumptions.

Not all of the benefits of Section 121 are enjoyed by older homeowners who move, although assigning monetary values to these additional effects is beyond the scope of this research. Three sets of beneficial effects seem clear. First, increased mobility by older homeowners opens up additional housing alternatives for younger households in search of larger owner-occupied homes. Section 121, then, produces at least two rounds of benefits: in the first round, older owners derive financial benefits in the form of tax forgiveness; in the second round, younger households in need of larger residences have their housing alternatives increased. (This chain of moves is, of course, only speculative. It would be extremely worthwhile to estimate how many links of this type actually exist. The Annual Housing Survey, which follows housing units over time, is ideally suited to such an analysis.)

The second positive effect of the exclusion results from benefits the mortgage industry derives from the turnover of below market rate mortages. We estimate that roughly 46 percent of owners who sold their primary residence after 1978 and were eligible for Section 121 benefits were still paying off a mortgage on that property, and the interest rate on that mortgage was roughly six percentage points below the going rate. Thrifts also derived benefits when homes owned free and clear were sold since the home sale allowed new, updated mortgages to be written on an inactive property. The financial benefits for thrift institutions from the rollover of below market mortgage interest rates will diminish over the long-term as the prevalance of fixed rate mortgages declines generally. But the time horizon over which these benefits will remain salient could be as long as 20 years.

The third benefit is derived by the real estate industry since the provision increases home sales activity.

It is not clear whether the distributional characteristics of Section 121 should be viewed positively or negatively. There is no question that the structure of the provision is regressive: the higher the income and the greater the accumulated gain, the greater the benefits. But probably because, on average, the current incomes of older owners (particularly those 65 and older) are low, the largest number of beneficiaries of Section 121 benefits in fact are middle-income. Furthermore, the value of tax savings derived from the provision hardly represents a windfall: the median value, in 1980 dollars, was only about $2,000 per year for movers 55 and older under the 1978 version. Thus, despite the inherent regressivity of the design of Section 121, the majority of its beneficiaries are middle-income homeowners and the size of the benefits they enjoy is modest.

The most questionable aspects of Section 121 concern its basic structure. The provision offers advantages only to homeowners, thereby discriminating in favor of older taxpayers who have been able to afford to own their home (Connealy, 1981). While the distributional implications of this policy are troublesome, it must also be remembered that more than three-quarters of all older households are homeowners, including a large proportion of very low-income households. Therefore, a provision that benefits older homeowners reaches a large fraction of the older population in households where the head is 65 or older. If the provision were more tightly targeted and designed to be more progressive, it might be a more attractive approach for increasing the mobility of older homeowners. Transfering benefits through the tax system also has the positive feature of administrative simplicity; further, low income older homeowners have demonstrated low participation rates in voucher-type housing programs. But developing criteria for tighter targeting cannot be pursued without further analysis of which households are most likely to undertake downgrading moves and, at the other extreme, which older households appear to be locked in their present residences and require assistance to move.

Another disturbing feature relates to a key premise on which Section 121 is based, namely, that older households have a strong desire to move to more manageable units and had been discouraged from doing so by, among other things, the bias in federal tax law toward upgrading. Our analysis suggests that even during the years in which one or another version of Section 121 was in effect, the moves made by older homeowners were not overwhelmingly downgrading moves. Even if Section

121 induced those moves that involved downgrading, this still would not necessarily indicate that the provision is effective. Such a positive characterization is only appropriate if those who are making the downgrading moves (and deriving the tax benefits of the provision) are also the intended beneficiaries of the assistance. If, for example, the fundamental goal of Section 121 is to assist older homeowners in the greatest financial need, there is strong evidence to suggest that they are not the policy's prime beneficiaries. Indeed, it is likely that older homeowners in the greatest need of financial assistance are those who do not (and perhaps cannot) move. Targeting assistance to those households could help them either better maintain their long-time housing units or move to units that are better suited to their needs. But if there is a shortage of appropriate housing alternatives for these households, no mobility incentive is likely to be very effective. This brings us back to the observation we made at the outset: the main objectives and primary beneficiaries of this provision were not clearly defined.

Closely related are some equity and efficiency concerns surrounding the age of eligibility for the provision. Since younger owners (here defined as 40 to 54 years old) do not differ substantially from those 55 to 64 in either the propensity to move or the tendency to upgrade or downgrade when selling a home, excluding them from Section 121 benefits cannot be justified on these substantive grounds, as appears to have been the case in the hearings on the Revenue Act of 1978. On the other hand, since, on average, those 55 to 64 years old have higher incomes, higher capital gains and, therefore, higher median tax savings from the provision, the extension of Section 121 benefits to them in the 1978 amendments more than doubled the revenue loss associated with the provison.

Modifying the age of eligibility for Section 121 has not, however, been included in recent proposals to alter the provision. In 1981, the Congressional Budget Office (1981) suggested reducing the excludable amount to $50,000 effective January 1, 1982. Connealy (1981) also favored reducing the excludable gain "...to $35,000 or some other reasonable amount," but further argued for reimposing a sales price limit and formula for excludable gain beyond that limit.

Each of these suggestions would somewhat reduce the revenue loss associated with the provision. The size of this effect is likely to be small, however: the estimates we derived on the median size of accumulated capital gain among those eligible for Section 121 indicate that a lower cap on the excludable gain would not adversely affect most older homeowners. Reimposing a sales price cap and formula would have a greater effect and would make the provision more progressive since the allowable amount of exclusion would decline as the sales price exceeded the threshold.

But both of these proposals represent relatively minor revisions to Section 121. Neither one addresses the more fundamental questions of identifying the key objectives of this provision and who should be its primary beneficiaries.

APPENDIX A
Legislative History of Section 121 of the Internal Revenue Code

Since 1951, the Internal Revenue Code has contained a rollover provision, Section 1034, that makes it easier for people to sell their homes in order to move into costlier housing (U.S. Senate, 1978a). In 1964, Section 121, an exclusion of capital gains on home sales for people 65 and over, was enacted in part to provide tax relief for elderly taxpayers who sell their homes to move to smaller units or apartments. (U.S. Senate, 1978a). Until 1976, all capital gains on a sale under $20,000 were excluded from gross income, and a portion of gains on sales exceeding $20,000--calculated by multiplying the gain by the ratio of $20,000 to the sales price--was also tax-exempt. The provision defined a principal residence as a home owned and occupied by the taxpayer for at least five of the eight years preceding the sale (U.S. Senate, 1976). The Tax Reform Act of 1976 raised the ceiling for a full exclusion to $35,000 in order to reflect the increase in the median sales price of a home since the provision was originally enacted. For a home sold for over $35,000, the exclusion was calculated as before by multiplying the gain by the ratio of $35,000 to the sales price in order to determine the tax-exempt gain. In its "Yellow Book" analysis of tax expenditures, the Congress recognized that Section 121 may provide an incidental incentive for older homeowners to wait until they reached aged 65 to put their homes on the market (U.S. Senate, 1978a).

Between 1976 and 1978, concerns about capital formation and capital mobility led to discussion of capital gains taxes in general. Special tax treatment for capital gains has traditionally been regarded as providing an incentive to increased personal saving, which in turn encourages capital growth. However, in hearings before the Subcommittee on Taxation and Debt Management of the Senate Committee on Finance, in response to questions from Senator Harry F. Byrd, Jr. (Virginia) and Senator Russell B. Long (Louisiana), Assistant Secretary of the Treasury for Economic Policy Daniel

Brill testified that tax incentives such as the capital gains provisions affect the form of saving rather than the net amount, and are therefore not a solution to the problem of personal saving shortfalls (U.S. Senate, 1977).

Nevertheless, a perception that capital gains taxes can be an unfair burden, promote "lock-in," restrict capital flow, and hamper capital formation, coupled with the recognition that the housing market had been particularly affected by inflation, apparently led to persistent pressure to alter capital gains treatment for home sales. There was also a perceived need to simplify this particularly complicated area of the tax laws (Joint Committee on Taxation, 1977a).

In the Ways and Means Committee, Section 405 of HR 13511, The Revenue Act of 1978 was drafted to amend Section 121 of the Code so that any taxpayer, regardless of age, could elect a once-in-a-lifetime exclusion of up to $100,000 of gain realized on the sale of a principal residence. A principal residence was redefined as a home owned and occupied by the taxpayer for at least two years leading up to the sale. In this draft, the provisions of Section 405 were not to be used in conjunction with those of Section 1034, meaning that accrued gains from prior home sales would not be exempted from taxes (U.S. House of Representatives, 1978).

This version of Section 405 followed proposed changes in Section 121 offered to the Committee by Representative Barber B. Conable, Jr. (New York) and Representative Richard T. Schulze (Pennsylvania). The Schulze proposal would have maintained the 65+ age limit, but eliminated any ceiling on the amount of capital gain exempt from taxation. Representative Conable suggested exclusion from adjusted gross income of all gains on sales of principal residences, with no age limit or dollar ceiling (Joint Committee on Taxation, 1978c). The version of Section 405 reported to the House and sent on to the Senate was only slightly more complicated and less generous than these proposed amendments.

HR 13511 was considered by the Senate in hearings before the Committee on Finance during August and September, 1978. W. Michael Blumenthal, Secretary of the Treasury, estimated the revenue loss that would result from the House version of Section 405 at $700 million (see Table A-1). He recommended cutting the loss to $300 million by imposing a $50,000 ceiling and limiting eligibility for the exclusion to individuals 55 and over, whom he believed to be the most likely to wish to downscale (U.S. Senate, 1978b). Blumenthal's recommendations received strong opposition from Senator Abraham Ribicoff (Connecticut) who felt that they biased the provision against younger and less wealthy people. Andrew Biemiller, representing the AFL-CIO, also argued that Section 405 was essentially a tax giveaway for the rich, but witnesses representing savings associations, realtors, homeowners, and retired persons spoke in favor of Section 405 as proposed, or in the slightly modified form (U.S. Senate, 1978b).

Blumenthal pointed out in his testimony that the needs of younger and lower-income homeowners are addressed in the capital gains rollover provisions of Section 1034 (U.S. Senate, 1978b). Thus, Section 121 was intended to be directed toward older taxpayers, and inclusion of an age limit in Section 405 would be appropriate.

The version of Section 405 that emerged from the Senate Committee provided for exclusion of all of the gain on homes sold for $50,000 or less. A formula was reintroduced for determination of the exclusion for sales exceeding $50,000: the fraction $50,000 divided by the selling price would be tax exempt. No age limit was imposed. The full Senate accepted this version, each chamber insisted on its own amendments, and a conference was called (U.S. Congress, 1978).

The conference committee agreed upon a version of Section 121 that established a $100,000 ceiling on the exclusion itself, regardless of sale price and without resort to formula and limited eligibility to taxpayers 55 or older. A principal residence was defined as a home owned and occupied by the taxpayer for at least three of the five years preceding the sale. Like the original Section 121 the conference version permitted individuals to use the exclusion in conjunction with the rollover provision, in effect creating a permanent forgiveness of accrued tax liabilities (U.S. Congress, 1978).

Both the House and the Senate accepted the conference report, which became Section 404 of the Revenue Act of 1978.[1] On November 6, 1978, the President signed the Act, and the new Section 404 amendments to Section 121 of the Code, into law.

---

[1] An attempt to insert an inflation adjustment for capital assets into the Section 404 amendments failed before the final version was set.

Table A-1

Fiscal Year Estimates of Revenue
Losses Associated With Section 121
(millions of dollars)

	Cost Estimates												
Original Section 121 (65+)	1975	1976	1977	1978	1979	1980	1981	1982	1983	1984	1985	1986	1987
Special Analysis G[a] (latest figure)	40	40	40	70	70								
"Yellow Book"[b]	40	45	50	70	70	70							
House Proposal (No Age Limit)													
Blumenthal[c]					700								
National Assoc. of Manufacturers[d]					745	820	901	992	1091				
Final Version (55+)													
Special Analysis G[a]					225	535	600	635	820				
"Yellow Book"[b]								510	550	675	830	1005	1175
Blumenthal[c]					300								
Church[e]					322								
Joint Committee[f]					165	415			522				

---

[a] "Special Analysis of the Budget." Analysis G, Editions 1975-1978.

[b] "Tax Expenditures." Committee Print, U.S. Senate Committee on the Budget, Editions 1976-1978.

[c] "Revenue Act of 1978." Hearings, U.S. Senate Committee on Finance, August-September 1978, p. 141.

[d] "Tax Expenditures." Committee Print, U.S. Senate Committee on the Budget. Edition 1982.

[e] Congressional Record, S17916, Oct. 10, 1978.

[f] Joint Committee on Taxation. (1979). General Explanation of Revenue Act of 1978, March 12. Washington, D.C.: Government Printing Office.

APPENDIX B
Explanation of Variables

I. Policy Variables, "Tax Savings"

The tax savings variable is the policy variable used in our analysis. It also provides an estimate of the revenue loss resulting from Section 121. The variable was constructed for each household in each year of our analysis whether or not the household sold their home. It represents the potential reduction in tax liability attributable to the home equity capital gains exclusion provision in effect at the time, if the household had sold their home during the year and not rolled the capital gain over to another home. Households which do not meet the age or residency requirements for the exclusion thus are assigned zero values. The magnitude of the variable for other households then is roughly a function of the specific provision in effect at the time, the taxable portion of capital gains on the home, and the household's marginal tax rate.

The construction of this variable is best understood by decomposing it into a series of component equations:[1]

$$\text{TAX SAVINGS} = ATL_{w/o} - ATL_{w} \qquad \text{(B-1)}$$

where $ATL_{w/o}$ = additional tax liability which would result from the sale of the home, assuming the capital gain is not rolled over to another home and assuming the absence of any home equity capital gains exclusion provisions in the tax code.

ATL_{w} = additional tax liability which would result from the sale of the home, given the home

---

[1] In our mobility model, we estimated the impact of Section 121 on moves that took place between pairs of consecutive years, from t-1 to t. The tax savings variable was calculated on the basis of conditions that existed at the start of year t-1.

equity capital gains exclusion provisions in effect at the time, and assuming the capital gains is not rolled over to another home.

The ATL variables were in turn calculated as the additional taxable income that would result from the sale of the home (assuming the non-existence and existence of the exclusion provisions in effect at the time respectively) times the household's marginal tax rate. The PSID provides an estimate of each household's marginal tax rate. This variable is based on the number of exclusions the household can claim, filing status and the taxable base income of the household.[2] Since the sale of a home may significantly increase the household's taxable income, it may also push the household into a significantly higher tax bracket. To allow for this, the additional taxable income from a home sale is multiplied by the average of the marginal tax rate the household would face in the absence of a home sale, and the marginal tax rate of the household in the hypothetical event of a home sale, with or without capital gains exclusion provisions in effect. These hypothetical marginal tax rates were assigned based on tax tables obtained from Lasser (1970-81):

$$\begin{aligned} ATL_{w/o} &= \left(\frac{MTR_1 + MTR_2}{2}\right)(\lambda - CG) \\ ATL_{w} &= \left(\frac{MTR_1 + MTR_3}{2}\right)(\lambda - (CG - TFCG)) \end{aligned} \qquad \text{(B-2)}$$

where MTR_1 = household's marginal tax rate if taxable income did not include capital gains from home sale.

MTR_2 = household's marginal tax rate if taxable income included taxable portion of capital gains from a home sale assuming the absence of any special exclusion of home equity capital gains.

MTR_3 = household's marginal tax rate if taxable income included taxable portion of capital gains from a home sale, given the special exclusion provisions in effect at the time.

---

[2] The PSID calculated marginal tax rates since interview year 1976. Prior to that, marginal tax rates were assigned to households based on filing status and estimated tax payments, a variable contained in the PSID.

λ = taxable portion of all capital gains. Fifty percent of capital gains were taxed from 1970 through 1978. After that, 40 percent were taxed.

CG = capital gains accrued on home.

TFCG = tax free capital gains resulting from special exclusion in effect at the time.

The construction of the CG variable was based on market house values reported by the respondents. In the first year of the PSID (1968) households were asked when they moved into their current home. For homeowners, the capital gain up to 1968 was calculated based on the average appreciation in house prices since the home was purchased. After 1968, the capital gains on the home was calculated as the previous year's capital gain plus (or minus) an amount equal to the change in the reported house value from the previous year. If the home was sold and the household moved into another owner-occupied home the following year, the capital gain was carried over to the new home.[3] Since the variable was constructed on the basis of the household head's perception of the current value of the home, some error may be introduced into the variable. Thus this variable actually reflects subjective perceptions which may differ from actual values.

A number of other measurement problems that arose in constructing the policy variable should also be noted. First, increases in house value may be attributable in part to improvements made to the home. The value of such improvements would be reflected in the basis of the home and should not be included as capital gains. Since the PSID does not contain any information concerning the value of improvements made to the home it was impossible for us to exclude these. Another source of error is the lack of information concerning any

---

[3] During most of the period of our analysis, capital gains could be rolled over if another home was purchased within 18 months of the sale of a home. Thus it is conceivable that a household that owned a home in one year, rented the following year, and then owned a home in the third year might have been able to roll over the capital gain. Our data do not allow for this determination, so we assumed that if a household reported renting at any interview, capital gains were not rolled over. The potential error in our estimate of capital gains is likely to be very small.

homes which may have been owned prior to the dwelling owned in 1968.

The tax free capital gain variable (TFCG) is defined differently in different years of our analysis, depending on the specific provisions concerning the treatment of capital gains on home equity in effect at the time. From the first year of our data file to 1976, households with the head or spouse age 65 or over qualified for an exclusion of capital gains if they resided in their principal dwelling five of the previous eight years. If the adjusted sale price of the home was $20,000 or less, the entire capital gain was excluded from gross income.[4] If the adjusted sale price was over $20,000, then the amount of the capital gain which could be excluded from gross income was:

$$TFCG = \left(\frac{\$20,000}{ASP}\right) \times CG \qquad \text{(B-3)}$$

where ASP = adjusted sales price.

This formula limited the exclusion to $20,000.

In 1977 and through the first half of 1978 the limit was raised to $35,000, but the method of calculation remained the same. Thus, all capital gains were excluded from gross income if the adjusted sales price was $35,000 or less: if it was greater than $35,000, the excluded portion was calculated using a formula similar to A-3, except that $35,000 replaced the $20,000 value.

Beginning in July 1978 and continuing through 1981 (the last year in our analysis file), the Section 404 amendments to Section 121 were in effect. To qualify: (1) either the head or spouse must be age 55 or over; (2) the home must have been used as their principal residence three of the previous five years; and (3) the excludable amount was raised to $100,000, regardless of sales price. Thus, TFCG simply equals CG up to a limit of $100,000.

---

[4] Adjusted sales price equals the actual sales price of the home minus the cost of selling the home (realtor fees, legal fees, and any fixing up costs required for the sale). This was approximated by the reported house value.

II. Price Discount[5]

Homeowners who hold fixed rate mortgages with interest rates lower than current mortgage interest rates enjoy lower housing costs than those who purchase an identical house at current mortgage rates. As a result, moving involves a substantial increase in the price households must pay for housing. This "price discount" on current homes may discourage some households from moving. The variable measures the degree to which households enjoy price discounts on their current homes (at time t-1).

The variable is constructed as the ratio of the after-tax user cost of a dollar's worth of the household's current housing over the after-tax user cost of a dollar's worth of newly purchased and mortgaged housing. The unit user cost of housing represents the price of housing when housing markets are in equilibrium. This variable, then, can be thought of as the ratio of the prices on the currently owned and contemporarily financed house.

The per unit after-tax user cost of housing is calculated as:

$$d + (1-m)[qi + (1-q)r + t] - n$$

where d = rate of gross depreciation (includes normal repair and maintenance costs plus depreciation of housing), assumed to be .025 for all homes

m = household's marginal tax rate

q = ratio of remaining mortgage principal to house value

i = mortgage interest rate

r = interest rate on alternative similar investments (AAA bond rate on 30-year corporate bonds used)

t = property tax rate (calculated as reported property tax payments over reported house value)

n = rate of expected inflation (calculated as weighted average of the rate of inflation in the current and previous two years).

The price discount variable for each household is calculated as:

$$\frac{d + (1-m)\ [qi^* + (1-q)r + t] - n}{d + (1-m)\ [.75i + .25r + t] - n}$$

---

[5] Adapted from Reschovsky (1982).

where i^* = the prevailing mortgage interest rate in the year the current home was purchased.

The denominator represents the after tax user cost of a home purchased in the current year. The use of .75 and .25 as q and (1-q), respectively, represents the average loan to house value for home sales. This ratio remained fairly constant over the period of this study.

The lower the value of the price discount variable, the greater the financial motivation to remain immobile. Therefore, we hypothesize this variable to be positively related to the probability of moving. Those households that purchased their homes when interest rates were significantly lower and still have a large portion of the house value in mortgage debt will enjoy the greatest discount. Most elderly homeowners own their homes free and clear of mortgage debt. Therefore, they are not likely to be major beneficiaries of these price discounts.

III. Specification of Variables Included in Logit Models

Dependent Variable:	(1) whether moved between year t-1 and t	moved = 1 else = 0
Independent Variables:	(1) # of rooms too many, t-1	actual # of rooms <u>more</u> than required based on age and sex of household members else = 0
	(2) # of rooms too few, t-1	actual # of rooms too few else = 0
	(3) change in family size, t-1 to t	actual # of persons added or subtracted from family unit
	(4) change in marital status, t-1 to t:	
	(a) remained married over period t-1 to t	remained married = 1 else = 0
	(b) remained single over period t-1 to t	remained single = 1 else = 0
	(c) experienced any change in marital status (e.g., single to married; married to single; other)	experienced change = 1 else = 0
	(5) lagged change in marital status t-2 to t-1	
	(a) remained married over period t-2 to t-1	remained married = 1 else = 0
	(b) remained single over period t-2 to t-1	remained single = 1 else = 0
	(c) experienced any change in marital status (e.g., single to married; married to single; other)	experienced change = 1 else = 0

(6)	change in retirement status:	
	(a) not retired, t-1; retired, t	not retired to retired = 1 else = 0
	(b) not retired, t-2; retired, t-1	not retired to retired = 1 else = 0
	(c) retired t-1	retired = 1 else = 0
(7)	age of head	continuous
(8)	sex of head	female = 1 else = 0
(9)	race	non-white = 1 else = 0
(10)	real income, t-1[1]	continuous
(11)	length of residence, t-1	continuous
(12)	price discount, t-1	continuous
(13)	unemployment rate, t-1	actual value
(14)	inflation rate, t-1	actual value
(15)	real interest rate, t-1	actual value
(16)	real tax savings[1]	continuous

[1] 1980 dollars, in thousands

APPENDIX C

Illustrative Calculations of Tax Savings Under Alternative Versions of Section 121[1]

---

[1]These examples are of tax savings at, or approaching, the maximum value under each of these versions of S.121.

I. <u>1964 Version of S.121</u> ($20,000 Exclusion)

<u>Example #1</u>

Adjusted sales price = $18,000

Basis on home = $10,000

Pre-sale adjusted gross income = $15,000
(assuming marginal tax rate of 25%)

$$CG = 18,000 - 10,000 = 8,000$$

$$TFCG = 8,000$$

$$ATL_{w/o} = (\frac{.25 + .28^{2}}{2}) \times .5^{3} \times 8000 - 1060$$

$$ATL_{w} = 0 \text{ (because all capital gains tax free)}$$

TAX SAVINGS = 1060 - 0 = $1060

<u>Example #2</u>

Adjusted sales price = $50,000

Basis on home = $25,000

Pre-sale adjusted gross income = $15,000

$$CG = 50,000 - 25,000 = 25,000$$

$$TFCG = (\frac{20,000}{50,000}) \times 25,000 = 10,000$$

$$ATL_{w/o} = (\frac{.25 + .32}{2})^{4} \times .5 \times 25,000 = \$3812.5$$

$$ATL_{w} = (\frac{.25 + .32}{2})^{5} \times .5 \times (25,000 - 10,000) = \$2137.5$$

TAX SAVINGS = 3812.5 - 2137.5 = $1675

---

[2] .28 (MTR_2) is marginal tax rate at $19,000, where $19,000 = $15,000 + taxable capital gains ($4,000).

[3] 50% of all long-term capital gains is taxed

[4] MTR at AGI = $27,500 (15,000 + (.5 x 25,000))

[5] MTR at AGI = $22,500 (15,000 + .5 x (25,000 - 10,000))

II. 1976 Version of S.121 ($35,000 Exclusion)

Example #1

Adjusted sales price = $50,000

Basis on home = $25,000

Pre-sale adjusted gross income = $15,000

$$CG = 50{,}000 - 25{,}000 = 25{,}000$$

$$TFCG = \left(\frac{35{,}000}{50{,}000}\right) \times 25{,}000 = 17{,}500$$

$$ATL_{w/o} = \left(\frac{.25 + .36}{2}\right) \times .5 \times 25{,}000 = \$3812.5$$

$$ATL_{w} = \left(\frac{.25 + .28}{2}\right) \times .5 \times (25{,}000 - 17{,}500) = \$\ 993.75$$

TAX SAVINGS = 3812.5 - 993.75 = $2818.75

III. 1978 Version of S.121 ($100,000 Exclusion)

Example #1

Adjusted sales price = $50,000

Basis on home = $25,000

Pre-sale adjusted gross income = $15,000

$$CG = 25{,}000$$

$$TFCG = 25{,}000$$

$$ATL_{w/o} = \left(\frac{.21 + .32}{2}\right) \times .4 \times 25{,}000 = \$2650$$

ATL_{w} = 0 (because all capital gains tax free)

TAX SAVINGS = $2650

Example #2

Adjusted sales price = \$200,000

Basis on home = \$50,000

Pre-sale adjusted gross income = \$250,000

CG = 150,000

TFCG = 100,000

$$ATL_{w/o} = \left(\frac{.7 + .7}{2}\right) \times .4 \times (150{,}000) = \$42{,}000$$

$$ATL_{w} = \left(\frac{.7 + .7}{2}\right) \times .4\ (150{,}000 - 100{,}000) = \$14{,}000$$

TAX SAVINGS = 42,000 - 14,000 = \$28,000

NOTE: In the 1979 interview year (i.e., homes sold in latter part of 1978), capital gains were taxed at 50 percent so that in the above example, the taxsavings would be larger:

$$ATL_{w/o} = \$52{,}500$$

$$ATL_{w} = \$17{,}500$$

TAX SAVINGS = \$35,000

APPENDIX D

Logit Results

I. Method for Estimating the Effect of Section 121 on Mobility Rates

Making predictions from logit equations is not as straightforward as when using OLS. Here we illustrate how the predictions contained in Table 6 were calculated. Numbers for the 55 to 64 year old age group are used.

The logit equation we estimated takes the form:

$$\ln\left(\frac{P_i}{1-P_i}\right) = a + bTS_i + cX_i$$

where: ln = natural logrithm

P_i = probability of household i moving

a = constant term

b = coefficient estimates on the tax savings variable

TS = tax savings

c = vector of coefficients associated with x

X = vector of other predictor variables

The above equation can be rewritten as:

$$P_i = \frac{1}{1+e^{-(a+bTS_i+cX_i)}}$$

Setting all values of X at their means and setting TS to zero yields a predicted probability of moving of .026. Keeping values of X at their mean values and setting TS to 4.276, the average value for owners aged 55 to 64 in the period 1978-80 (recall that TS is measured in thousands of dollars), yields a predicted mobility rate of .030. The difference between these two predictions, .004, represents our estimate of the marginal impact of the provision.

II. Population Mean Values on Independent Variables Used to Estimate Size of Section 121 Effects

Variable	Mean Value: All Age Groups Pooled	Mean Value: 55 - 64 Year Olds	Mean Value: 65 or Older
Tax Savings (real dollars)	.7754	1.5165	1.1411
Marital Status Change, T-1 to T:			
Married, no change	.7278	.7379	.5570
Single, no change	.2329	.2368	.3813
Any change	.0393	.0253	.0617
Marital Status Change, T-2 to T-1:			
Married, no change	.7439	.7466	.5834
Single, no change	.2196	.2213	.3605
Any change	.0366	.0321	.0561
Length of Residence	15.1694	16.4282	19.2503
# of Rooms too Many	3.0520	3.2553	3.1919
# of Rooms too Few	.0221	.0144	--[a]
Price Discount	.7592	.7488	.8242
Change in Family Size	.1126	.0983	.0431
Female Head	.2204	.2282	.3513
Non-White Head	.0913	.0846	.0818
Age of Head	58.8459	59.8741	73.3555
Unemployment Rate	6.4059	6.4397	6.4190
Inflation Rate	8.2809	8.3267	8.5033
Real Interest Rate	.0270	.0269	.0276
Real Income	24.5683	25.2135	13.7650
Change in Retirement Status:			
Not Retired, T-1; Retired, T	.0399	.0537	.0534
Not Retired, T-2; Retired, T-1	.0364	.0386	.0786
Retired, T-1	.2369	.0819	.7110

[a]Because there were no cases of persons 65 or older with too few rooms, this variable was deleted from this run.

LOGIT FOR ALL AGE GROUPS

TABLE OF COEFFICIENTS
BASED ON POPULATION WEIGHTED DATA
** WARNING: STANDARD ERRORS ARE BEING CALCULATED
WITH POPULATION WEIGHTED DATA

VAR #	PARTIAL (%)	MODEL 2 B	STANDARD ERROR	(B/SE)	MODEL 1 B	VARIABLE NAME
V0	0.0	-0.8017	0.1416	(-5.66)	-3.2848	CONSTANT
V158	0.2	0.0500	0.0028	(17.89)	0.0000	REAL TAX SAVINGS
R150	0.7	(CHISQ=1184.46	2 DF)			MAR CHG T-1 TO T
CAT 1	0.0	0.0521	0.0154	(3.37)	0.0000	
CAT 2	0.0	-0.3168	0.0463	(-6.84)	0.0000	
CAT 3	0.5	0.9136	0.0308	(29.64)	0.0000	
R151	0.3	(CHISQ= 501.02	2 DF)			MAR CHG T-2 TO T-1
CAT 1	0.3	-0.3024	0.0135	(-22.34)	0.0000	
CAT 2	0.3	0.9572	0.0435	(21.98)	0.0000	
CAT 3	0.1	0.4050	0.0366	(11.06)	0.0000	
V105	1.3	-0.0416	0.0009	(-48.50)	0.0000	DUR OF RES, T-1
V107	0.3	0.1145	0.0054	(21.06)	0.0000	# RMS TOO MANY, T-1
V108	0.1	0.4249	0.0288	(14.74)	0.0000	# RMS TOO FEW, T-1
V115	0.0	0.2689	0.0459	(5.86)	0.0000	PRICE DISCOUNT, T-1
V148	0.0	0.0365	0.0135	(2.70)	0.0000	CHG IN FAM SIZE
V151	0.3	-0.6753	0.0284	(-23.80)	0.0000	FEMALE HEAD
V152	0.3	-0.8689	0.0365	(-23.80)	0.0000	NON WHITE
V21	0.2	-0.0212	0.0010	(-20.36)	0.0000	AGE OF HEAD
R113	0.0	-0.1273	0.0169	(-7.55)	0.0000	UNEMPL RT,T-1
R114	0.0	-0.0297	0.0044	(-6.75)	0.0000	INFLAT RT,T-1
V153	0.1	-0.0069	0.0005	(-13.42)	0.0000	REAL INC,T-1
R100	0.5	0.9197	0.0310	(29.63)	0.0000	NOT RET-RET
R101	0.0	0.3087	0.0398	(7.75)	0.0000	NOT RET-RET,T-1
R102	0.0	0.1619	0.0281	(5.77)	0.0000	RETIRED,T-1
R55	0.0	-1.2209	1.4864	(-0.82)	0.0000	REAL INT RATE,T-1

ANALYSIS OF PREDICTIVE POWER FOR THE REGRESSION
USING POPULATION WEIGHTED DATA

PROPORTION OF Y=1 IN POPULATION 0.036

	NO OF PARAMETERS	PREDICTIVE POWER	"ADJUSTED" PREDP
MODEL 0	1	0.856	0.856
MODEL 2	21	0.863	0.862

SOURCE	PREDICTION ERROR	PERCENT OF TOTAL	DF	SUM OF SQUARES	PERCENT OF TOTAL
DUE TO MODEL2	0.007	4.8	20	464.9	2.5
MODEL 2 ERROR	0.137	95.2		18,412.2	97.5
MODEL 0 ERROR(TOTAL)	0.144	100.0	20	18,877.1	100.0

LOGIT FOR 55-64

TABLE OF COEFFICIENTS
BASED ON POPULATION WEIGHTED DATA
** WARNING: STANDARD ERRORS ARE BEING CALCULATED
WITH POPULATION WEIGHTED DATA

VAR #	PARTIAL (%)	MODEL 2 B	STANDARD ERROR	(B/SE)	MODEL 1 B	VARIABLE NAME
VO	0.3	-5.1109	0.4647	(-11.00)	-3.3652	CONSTANT
V158	0.2	0.0335	0.0040	(8.36)	0.0000	REAL TAX SAVINGS
R150	1.7	(CHISQ=	618.12	2 DF)		MAR CHG T-1 TO T
CAT 1	0.3	0.3514	0.0359	(9.78)	0.0000	
CAT 2	0.3	-1.2151	0.1086	(-11.19)	0.0000	
CAT 3	0.7	1.1272	0.0712	(15.83)	0.0000	
R151	1.2	(CHISQ=	427.85	2 DF)		MAR CHG T-2 TO T-1
CAT 1	1.1	-0.6116	0.0297	(-20.61)	0.0000	
CAT 2	1.1	1.9899	0.0982	(20.27)	0.0000	
CAT 3	0.1	0.5058	0.0798	(6.34)	0.0000	
V105	0.7	-0.0270	0.0017	(-16.04)	0.0000	DUR OF RES, T-1
V107	0.2	0.0896	0.0120	(7.46)	0.0000	# RMS TOO MANY, T-1
V108	0.3	0.7895	0.0770	(10.26)	0.0000	# RMS TOO FEW, T-1
V115	0.0	-0.2957	0.0950	(-3.11)	0.0000	PRICE DISCOUNT, T-1
V148	0.3	0.2841	0.0283	(10.03)	0.0000	CHG IN FAM SIZE
V151	0.5	-0.8783	0.0646	(-13.59)	0.0000	FEMALE HEAD
V152	0.3	-0.8413	0.0842	(-10.00)	0.0000	NON WHITE
V21	0.0	0.0222	0.0065	(3.43)	0.0000	AGE OF HEAD
R113	0.1	0.1425	0.0326	(4.37)	0.0000	UNEMPL RT,T-1
R114	0.2	-0.0801	0.0102	(-7.89)	0.0000	INFLAT RT,T-1
V153	0.0	-0.0041	0.0011	(-3.74)	0.0000	REAL INC,T-1
R100	0.5	0.7809	0.0584	(13.37)	0.0000	NOT RET-RET
R101	0.1	-0.5305	0.0989	(-5.36)	0.0000	NOT RET-RET,T-1
R102	0.4	0.7467	0.0638	(11.71)	0.0000	RETIRED,T-1
R55	0.1	20.0029	3.0476	(6.56)	0.0000	REAL INT RATE,T-1

ANALYSIS OF PREDICTIVE POWER FOR THE REGRESSION
USING POPULATION WEIGHTED DATA

PROPORTION OF Y=1 IN POPULATION 0.033

	NO OF PARAMETERS	PREDICTIVE POWER	"ADJUSTED" PREDP
MODEL 0	1	0.864	0.864
MODEL 2	21	0.872	0.869

SOURCE	PREDICTION ERROR	PERCENT OF TOTAL	DF	SUM OF SQUARES	PERCENT OF TOTAL
DUE TO MODEL2	0.008	5.8	20	172.4	4.3
MODEL 2 ERROR	0.128	94.2		3,845.7	95.7
MODEL 0 ERROR(TOTAL)	0.136	100.0	20	4,018.2	100.0

LOGIT FOR 65+

TABLE OF COEFFICIENTS
BASED ON POPULATION WEIGHTED DATA
** WARNING: STANDARD ERRORS ARE BEING CALCULATED
WITH POPULATION WEIGHTED DATA

VAR #	PARTIAL (%)	MODEL 2 B	STANDARD ERROR	(B/SE)	MODEL 1 B	VARIABLE NAME
V0	0.5	-4.3491	0.3085	(-14.10)	-3.4629	CONSTANT
V158	0.2	0.0623	0.0067	(9.32)	0.0000	REAL TAX SAVINGS
R150	0.5	(CHISQ= 220.21		2 DF)		MAR CHG T-1 TO T
CAT 1	0.4	-0.6585	0.0478	(-13.77)	0.0000	
CAT 2	0.4	0.9226	0.0712	(12.95)	0.0000	
CAT 3	0.0	0.2437	0.0563	(4.32)	0.0000	
R151	0.5	(CHISQ= 223.74		2 DF)		MAR CHG T-2 TO T-1
CAT 1	0.4	0.5845	0.0466	(12.55)	0.0000	
CAT 2	0.4	-0.9429	0.0703	(-13.41)	0.0000	
CAT 3	0.0	-0.0185	0.0628	(-0.29)	0.0000	
V105	1.0	-0.0276	0.0013	(-20.59)	0.0000	DUR OF RES, T-1
V107	0.3	0.1211	0.0112	(10.81)	0.0000	# RMS TOO MANY, T-1
V115	0.0	0.1775	0.1383	(1.28)	0.0000	PRICE DISCOUNT, T-1
V148	0.2	0.2614	0.0319	(8.20)	0.0000	CHG IN FAM SIZE
V151	0.1	0.2670	0.0520	(5.13)	0.0000	FEMALE HEAD
V152	0.3	-0.9280	0.0800	(-11.60)	0.0000	NON WHITE
V21	0.1	0.0160	0.0027	(5.98)	0.0000	AGE OF HEAD
R113	0.1	-0.1779	0.0296	(-6.01)	0.0000	UNEMPL RT,T-1
R114	0.2	0.0758	0.0091	(8.30)	0.0000	INFLAT RT,T-1
V153	0.0	-0.0009	0.0008	(-1.14)	0.0000	REAL INC,T-1
R100	1.4	1.3995	0.0568	(24.62)	0.0000	NOT RET-RET
R101	0.5	0.6852	0.0486	(14.11)	0.0000	NOT RET-RET,T-1
R102	0.1	0.2783	0.0434	(6.42)	0.0000	RETIRED,T-1
R55	0.1	-14.9897	2.7911	(-5.37)	0.0000	REAL INT RATE,T-1

ANALYSIS OF PREDICTIVE POWER FOR THE REGRESSION
USING POPULATION WEIGHTED DATA

PROPORTION OF Y=1 IN POPULATION 0.030

	NO OF PARAMETERS	PREDICTIVE POWER	"ADJUSTED" PREDP
MODEL 0	1	0.873	0.873
MODEL 2	20	0.879	0.877

SOURCE	PREDICTION ERROR	PERCENT OF TOTAL	DF	SUM OF SQUARES	PERCENT OF TOTAL
DUE TO MODEL2	0.006	4.9	19	111.0	2.4
MODEL 2 ERROR	0.121	95.1		4,590.2	97.6
MODEL 0 ERROR(TOTAL)	0.127	100.0	19	4,701.2	100.0

#654493

APPENDIX E

Tables

Table E-1

Proportion of Moves to Smaller Dwellings,[a]
By Age and Year
(movers who remained owners)

Age	Year 1969-76	1977	1978-80
40 - 54 years old	.28	.37	.37
(N)	(182)	(32)	(53)
55 - 64 years old	.24	--	.35
(N)	(73)		(35)
65 or older	.35	--	.49
(N)	(56)		(32)

[a]Measured by number of rooms in the dwelling. Dwellings of equal size were included with larger dwellings.

-- Insufficient cases.

5.5

Table E-2

Mean Change in Number of Rooms
Between Pre- and Post-Move Year,
By Age and Year
(movers who remained owners)

Year	Year 1969-76	1977	1978-80
40 - 54 years old	.09	--	-.42
(N)	(182)		(53)
55 - 64 years old	-.06	--	.04
(N)	(73)		(35)
65 or older	-.36	--	-.53
(N)	(56)		(32)

-- Insufficient cases.

5.4a

Table E-3

Post-Move Tenure for Sellers 65 and Older
Under Alternative Tax Provisions,
By Amount of Real[a] Tax Savings

Post-Move Tenure	Tax Savings 0	< $3500	$3500 or more
1969 - 76			
Own	66.5%	62.1%	--
Rent	31.3	27.5	--
Neither	2.3	10.5	--
	100.0%	100.0%	--
(N)	(33)	(65)	--
1978 - 80			
Own	61.8%	75.1%	88.0%
Rent	19.4	23.9	12.0
Neither	18.8	1.0	...
	100.0%	100.0%	100.0%
(N)	(21)	(18)	(12)

[a]1980 dollars.

... Zero cases.

-- Insufficient cases.

#618076

Table E-4

Post-Move Tenure of Section 121 Beneficiaries,
By Amount of Real[a] Tax Savings and Age
(movers in 1978 - 80 only)

	Tax Savings		
Post-Move Tenure	0	< $3500	$3500 or more
55 - 64 years old			
Own	81.3%	77.8%	81.8%
Rent	18.7	22.2	9.0
Neither	...	...	9.3
	100.0%	100.0%	100.0%
(N)	(11)	(20)	(19)
65 or older			
Own	61.8%	75.1%	88.0%
Rent	19.4	23.9	12.0
Neither	18.8	1.0	...
	100.0%	100.0%	100.0%
(N)	(21)	(18)	(12)

[a] 1980 dollars

... Zero cases.

#618076

Table E-5

Simulated Real[a] Tax Savings Under Section 121,
By Age and Income
(nonmovers in 1978 - 80 only)

Tax Savings	Income[b]			
55 - 64 years old:	< $10,000	$10,000-19,999	$20,000-39,999	$40,000 or more
$0	33.3%	20.9%	12.2%	9.6%
< $3500	59.3	59.4	37.8	14.6
$3500 or more	7.5	19.7	50.0	75.8
	100.0%	100.0%	100.0%	100.0%
(N)	(304)	(398)	(528)	(190)
				tau-b=.388 tau-c=.386
65 or older:				
$0	38.6%	18.7%	14.6%	5.3%
< $3500	57.3	67.6	48.6	7.1
$3500 or more	4.1	13.6	36.8	87.6
	100.0%	100.0%	100.0%	100.0%
(N)	(786)	(455)	(231)	(54)
				tau-b=.371 tau-c=.338

[a]1980 dollars.

[b]Net of proceeds from home sale.

#618076

Table E-6

Simulated Real[a] Tax Savings Under Alternative Tax Provisions for Homeowners 65 or Older, By Income (nonmovers)

Tax Savings	Income[b]			
1969 - 76[c]	< $10,000	$10,000-19,999	$20,000-39,999	$40,000 or more
$0	24.4%	27.9%	18.7%	6.2%
< $3500	75.1	69.4	77.8	74.5
$3500 or more	.5	2.6	3.5	19.3
	100.0%	100.0%	100.0%	100.0%
(N)	(1331)	(796)	(340)	(82)
				tau-b=.070 tau-c=.052
1978 - 81[d]				
$0	38.6%	18.7%	14.6%	5.3%
< $3500	57.3	67.6	48.6	7.1
$3500 or more	4.1	13.6	36.8	87.6
	100.0%	100.0%	100.0%	100.0%
(N)	(786)	(455)	(231)	(54)
				tau-b=.371 tau-c=.338

[a] 1980 dollars.

[b] Net of proceeds from home sale.

[c] $20,000 exclusion (see text for details).

[d] $100,000 exclusion (see text for details).

#618076

References

Congressional Budget Office. (1981). The Tax Treatment of Homeownership: Issues and Options. Washington, D.C.: U.S. Government Printing Office.

Connealy, C. (1981). "Tax Consequences on the Disposition of a Personal Residence." University of Missouri-Kansas City Law Review, Winter, 137-157.

Executive Office of the President of the U.S., Annual Reports (1970-1984). Special Analyses: Budget of the U.S. Government. Washington, D.C.: Executive Office of the President, Office of Management and Budget.

Harney, Kenneth R. (1980). "A Tax-Exempt Bonanza." The Washington Post, February 2.

Harney, Kenneth R. (1980). "The Twists and Turns of a $100,000 Tax Break." The Washington Post, February 9.

Internal Revenue Code. (1951). S.1034.

Internal Revenue Code. (1964). S.121.

Irwin, Robert. (1981). The $100,000 Decision. New York: McGraw Hill Book Company.

Joint Committee on Taxation. (1982). Estimates of Federal Tax Expenditures for Fiscal Years 1982-1987, March 8. Washington, D.C.: U.S. Government Printing Office.

Joint Committee on Taxation. (1979). General Explanation of the Revenue Act of 1978, March 12. Washington, D.C.: U.S. Government Printing Office.

Joint Committee on Taxation. (1977a). Issues in Simplification of the Income Tax Laws, September. Washington, D.C.: U.S. Government Printing Office.

Joint Committee on Taxation. (1978a). Section-By-Section Summary of the Revenue Act of 1978 (P.L. 95-600;H.R. 13511), November 27. Washington, D.C.: U.S. Government Printing Office.

Joint Committee on Taxation. (1978b). Summary of Testimony on H.R. 13511 (The Revenue Act of 1978), September 7. Washington, D.C.: U.S. Government Printing Office.

Joint Committee on Taxation. (1977b). Tax Policy and Capital Formation, April 4. Washington, D.C.: U.S. Government Printing Office.

Joint Committee on Taxation. (1978c). Tax Reduction and Reform Proposals (Pt. 4: Alternative Capital Gains Tax), April 18. Washington, D.C.: U.S. Goverment Printing Office.

Lasser Institute. (1970-81). Your Income Tax. New York: Prentice Hall.

Morgan, James N. (1972). A Panel Study of Income Dynamics: Study Design, Procedures, Available Data, Vol. I. Ann Arbor: Institute for Social Research.

Morgan, James N. (1979). "Memo on Representativeness of the Panel Study of Income Dynamics." Ann Arbor: Institute for Social Research.

Nelson, Gary M. (1983). "Tax Expenditures for the Elderly." The Gerontologist, Vol. 23, No. 5, 471-478.

Newman, Sandra and Reschovsky, James. (1984). "An Evaluation of the One-Time Capital Gains Exclusion for Older Homeowners." Paper prepared for presentation at the Sixth Annual Association for Public Policy Analysis and Management Research Conference, New Orleans, Louisiana.

President's Commission on Housing. (1982). The Report of the President's Commission on Housing. Washington, D.C.: President's Commission on Housing.

Reschovsky, J. (1982). Aging in Place: An Investigation of the Housing Consumption and Residential Mobility of the Elderly. Ann Arbor, Michigan: Doctoral Dissertation in Public Policy Studies.

U.S. Department of Commerce, Bureau of the Census. (1982). Household and Family Characteristics: March, 1982. Current Population Reports, Series P-20, No. 381. Washington, D.C.: U.S. Government Printing Office.

U.S. Department of the Treasury. (1984a). Personal communications with Internal Revenue Service, Statistics on Income Division.

U.S. Department of the Treasury. (1984b). Personal communications with Office of Tax Analysis.

U.S. House of Representatives, Committee on Ways and Means. (1978). Summary of H.R. 13511, The Revenue Act of 1978, July. Washington, D.C.: Committee on Ways and Means.

U.S. Senate, Committee on the Budget. (1976). Tax Expenditures -- Compendium of Background Material on Individual Provisions, March 17. Washington, D.C.: U.S. Government Printing Office.

U.S. Senate, Committee on the Budget. (1978a). Tax Expenditures -- Relationships to Spending Programs and Background Material on Individual Provisions, September. Washington, D.C.: Committee on the Budget.

U.S. Senate, Committee on Finance. (1978b). Hearings Before the Committee on Finance--U.S. Senate 95th Congress Second Session on H.R.13511, Pt. 1 - 6, August 17, 21-25, September 6. Washington, D.C.: Committee on Finance.

U.S. Senate, Subcommittee on Taxation and Debt Management Generally. (1977). Incentives for Economic Growth, May and June. Washington, D.C.: Committee on Finance.

U.S. Congress, House Information System. (1984). 95th Congress Status Profile: H.R. 13511.

U.S. Congress, Senate. (1978). Congressional Record, October 10, S17916-S17920.

ISR RESEARCH REPORTS

The following Research Reports have been published by ISR. They are available in paperbound editions only. For information on prices and availability, write to the ISR Publishing Division, P.O. Box 1248, Ann Arbor, Michigan 48106.

Tranquilizer Use and Well-Being: A Longitudinal Study of Social and Psychological Effects. Robert D. Caplan, Antoina Abbey, David J. Abramis, Frank M. Andrews, Terry L. Conway, and John R. P. French, Jr. 1984. 442 pp.

Career Change in Midlife: Stress, Social, Support, and Adjustment. John R. P. French, Jr., Steven R. Doehrman, Mary Lou Davis-Sacks, and Amiram Vinokur. 1983. 152 pp.

Compensating for Missing Survey Data. Graham Kalton. 1983. 164 pp.

Residential Displacement in the U.S., 1970-1977. Sandra J. Newman and Michael S. Owen. 1982. 98 pp.

Sex Role Attitudes among High School Seniors: Views about Work and Family Life. A. Regula Herzog and Jerald G. Bachman. 1982. 272 pp.

Subjective Well-Being among Different Age Groups. A. Regula Herzog, Willard L. Rodgers, and Joseph Woodworth. 1982. 115 pp.

Employee Ownership. Michael Conte, Arnold S. Tannenbaum, and Donna McCulloch. 1981. 70 pp.

Recreation and Quality of Urban Life: Recreational Resources, Behaviors, and Evaluations of People in the Detroit Region. Robert W. Marans and J. Mark Fly. 1981. 240 pp.

A Comparative Study of the Organization and Performance of Hospital Emergency Services. Basil S. Georgopoulos and Robert A. Cooke. 1980. 512 pp.

An Evaluation of "Freestyle": A Television Series to Reduce Sex-Role Stereotypes. Jerome Johnston, James Ettema, and Terrence Davidson. 1980. 308 pp.

Occupational Stress and the Mental and Physical Health of Factory Workers. James S. House. 1980. 356 pp.

Job Demands and Worker Health: Main Effects and Occupational Differences. Robert D. Caplan, Sidney Cobb, John R. P. French, Jr., R. Van Harrison, and S. R. Pinneau, Jr. 1980. 342 pp.

Perceptions of Life Quality in Rural America: An Analysis of Survey Data from Four Studies. Robert W. Marans and Donald A. Dillman, with the assistance of Janet Keller. 1980. 118 pp.

Social Support and Patient Adherence: Experimental and Survey Findings. Robert D. Caplan, R. Van Harrison, Retha V. Wellons, and John R. P. French, Jr. 1980. 283 pp.

Working Together: A Study of Cooperation among Producers, Educators, and Researchers to Create Educational Television. James S. Ettema. 1980. 220 pp.

Experiments in Interviewing Techniques: Field Experiments in Health Reporting, 1971-1977. Edited by Charles F. Cannell, Lois Oksenberg, and Jean M. Converse. 1979. 446 pp.

The 1977 Quality of Employment Survey: Descriptive Statistics, with Comparison Data from the 1969-70 and 1972-73 Surveys. Robert P. Quinn and Graham L. Staines. 1979. 364 pp.

The Physical Environment and the Learning Process: A Survey of Recent Research. Jonathan King, Robert W. Marans, and associates. 1979. 92 pp.

Results of Two National Surveys of Philanthropic Activity. James N. Morgan, Richard F. Dye, and Judith H. Hybels. 1979. 204 pp.

A Survey of American Gambling Attitudes and Behavior. Maureen Kallick, Daniel Suits, Ted Dielman, and Judith Hybels. 1979. 560 pp.